The Family Christmas Cookbook

Best-Loved Recipes from *The Christmas Annual*

Augsburg Books

MINNEAPOLIS

Cover design by Michelle L. N. Cook; Cover art from Superstock
Interior design by Laurie Ingram
Text editing by Andrea Lee Schieber, Lois Wallentine, and Abby Coles
Recipe editing by Grace Wells

ISBN 0-8066-4802-3

The paper used in this publication meets the minimum requirements of American National Standard for Information Sciences—Permanence of Paper for Printed Library Materials, ANSI Z329.48-1985. ♾ ™

Manufactured in Canada

08	07	06	05	04	1	2	3	4	5	6	7	8	9	10

Permission Credits:
"Christmas Morning" by Jane Elkington Wohl, © 1993 Jane Elkington Wohl. Used by permission.
"A Cow's Eye View of Christmas" by Dawn Finlay, © 1991 Estate of Dawn Finlay. Used by permission.
Poem (untitled) by Cleoral Lovell, © 1993 Estate of Cleoral Lovell. Used by permission.

Table of Contents

Introduction

—•◆•—

What makes Christmas *Christmas?* Perhaps it is family and friends gathered for a meal or remembering holidays past or creating new traditions. *The Family Christmas Cookbook* not only offers recipes for tasty holiday breads, appetizers and main dishes, desserts, and cookies, but it also celebrates a rich heritage of Christmas traditions from around the world, featuring foods from Africa, Asia, Europe, Mexico, South America, and the United States.

The story or poem that accompanies each recipe represents another holiday tradition—*Christmas: The Annual of Christmas Literature and Art,* a yearly publication launched by Augsburg Publishing House (the predecessor to Augsburg Fortress, Publishers) in 1931 and published every Christmas for sixty-five years. The annual's editor and founder, Randolph E. Haugan, succinctly explained the publication's focus: "The greatest event in history was the coming of the Christ child." Indeed, *The Christmas Annual,* as it came to be known, brought the Christmas gospel, stories, poems, music, art, and traditional recipes to homes across the country and across generations.

Introduced during the Depression, *The Christmas Annual* heralded in the season. Upon receiving his copy of Volume 4, J. C. Penney, founder of the department store, foretold, "If all the issues are as fine as that for

1934, you may be successful in establishing the custom in the country." Eleanor Roosevelt wrote to the company in 1954, expressing "I always find that this adds much to our enjoyment during the holidayseason." In its lifetime, the annual reached thousands of homes and was a regular bestseller.

The Christmas Annual's legacy continues through this cookbook, as we celebrate Christ's birth through foods and traditions from around the world. While you bake German *honig kuchen,* a Christmassy-spiced cookie, you can read about German tree traditions. As you knead your *vörtlimpor,* you can learn about the Swedish custom of Dipping Day, which originated during a famine when people survived on only bread and broth. Many other traditional recipes will introduce you to gift-givers and customs from around the world, including the *Baboushka* in Russia, *Christkindli* in Switzerland, and the Three Kings in Mexico.

Just as spices give flavor to our favorite recipes, so too can diverse international traditions from long ago enliven our own holiday celebrations today. As a collection, the stories and recipes illustrate how we as a global family come together by God's hand and grow in the warmth of God's light.

Welcome, Christmas!

Ideas for Families

— • ◆ • —

Make your Christmas cooking and baking a family activity. Here are several suggestions for involving young children in the preparations of these treats. Be sure to adjust the activity to the age and ability of each child, keeping safety in mind.

Preparation

Invite a child to:

- Wash his or her hands.
- Put on an apron or wear a large, button-down shirt backwards. It might be fun for the helper to use an apron that once belonged to a special friend or family member.
- Grease baking pans or cookie sheets. Have your child use a clean paper towel, wax paper, or freshly washed hands to spread shortening, butter, or vegetable oil evenly into the pans.
- Clear space on a counter or a table for cooling cookies. Set out wire racks or tear and arrange sheets of wax paper.

Measuring and Mixing

Your child can:

- Fill measuring cups with flour or sugar. It might be helpful to pour the sugar or flour into a large plastic container or pan. Give your helper a spoon to fill the measuring cups and a flat-edged tool for leveling.
- Measure out other ingredients, such as salt, baking soda or powder, or vanilla. Have your child hold the measuring spoon over a larger dish to catch spillage.
- Break eggs into a separate bowl (so you can fish out any shells).
- Find the right measurement marking on butter or margarine wrappers where an adult or older child will make the cut.
- Stir in ingredients when hand mixing. For even mixing, you might want to switch off with your child; count ten stirs, then alternate turns.
- Take a turn at cutting in butter by hand or kneading or punching down bread dough. Again, for even mixing, you might want to switch off with your child; count to five or ten movements, then alternate turns.

Shaping and Preparing

Encourage your child to help you follow the recipe directions. A young person might assist with:

- Rolling bread dough into ropes or buns. For long ropes, have your child help you gently lift the dough.
- Weaving bread dough into braids or pretzel shapes.
- Sealing the ends of filled dough.

- Rolling cookie dough into balls.
- Dusting the rolling pin with flour.
- Rolling out dough to the desired thickness.
- Cutting out shapes with cookie cutters.
- Hiding an edible nut in the middle of the pudding or bread dough.

Power-Tool Safety

To clarify safety limits, you might:
- Consider restricting the use of a food processor or an electric mixer to older children or teens, especially if pouring in ingredients while the blade or beaters are moving or if needing to scrape the mixing bowl while it is running.
- Allow younger children to push buttons on safe appliances. With supervision, a blender can be a safer alternative to a food processor for some tasks. To chop nuts or fruit, have the child put the ingredients in the container, then place the cover on the blender. An adult should hold the container firmly on the unit as the child presses the "chop" button, then the "stop/off" button.

Finishing Touches

Invite your child to:
- Set timers for cooking or baking and keep watch through the oven door.
- Help read the thermometer to check the temperature of meat or liquids.
- Use a spatula to remove cookies from baking sheets and place them on cooling racks. (If the cookie sheet is hot, you may wish to do this yourself.)
- Sprinkle sugar, nut, or dried fruit toppings on cookies or breads.
- Drizzle glaze or spread icing on cookies.
- Package up baked goods once they have cooled.

Clean-up

Even young children can:
- Carry dirty utensils (except knives and sharp objects) and measuring cups to the sink.
- Brush flour, sugar, etc., from the table or counter into a wastebasket.
- Sweep the floor around the table or counter where you have been working.

Christmas *Morning*

by Jane Elkington Wohl

Spoons, reflections inverted in their bowls,
rest on the wooden cutting board.
A pile of soft, white linen towels
catches the light which presses toward
the fading night, as, mixing muffins, I
add eggs, nuts, and milk to flour,
that fine white dust which turns by
measured transformation into small, round loaves.

Light through the Eastern window kneads
the air until, within the quiet of the kitchen,
I rise in praise of all that feeds
the spirit and the flesh as well.
The kneading and the baking will combine
to nourish children, mine and thine.

From *Christmas: The Annual of Christmas Literature and Art*,
1993, volume 63, page 34

Gingerbread Pancakes

A Christmassy breakfast treat

Pancakes

3 cups all-purpose flour
6 teaspoons baking powder
3 teaspoons unsweetened baking cocoa
1 ½ teaspoons ground ginger
¾ teaspoon ground cinnamon
¾ teaspoon ground cloves
6 tablespoons ground hazelnuts, if desired
3 cups milk
6 tablespoons dark molasses
6 egg whites
1 to 2 tablespoons vegetable oil
Maple syrup or sweetened whipped cream, if desired

Special equipment

Gingerbread figure cookie cutter, optional

1. In large bowl, combine flour, baking powder, cocoa, ginger, cinnamon, cloves, and ground hazelnuts. In medium bowl, combine milk, molasses, and egg whites; beat well. Make a well in center of flour mixture. Add milk mixture; stir just until dry ingredients are moistened. (Batter will be lumpy.)

2. Heat oven to 200ºF. Heat oil in large nonstick skillet or on griddle over medium heat. For each pancake, spoon batter into pan to equal size of desired gingerbread figure cookie cutter. Cook about 2 minutes or until bubbles appear on top. Turn pancake; cook about 2 minutes. Press cookie cutter into each pancake. Discard trimmed pieces. If desired, place gingerbread pancakes on ovenproof plate; keep warm in oven. Serve with syrup or whipped cream.

Makes about 12 large pancakes.

From *Christmas: The Annual of Christmas Literature and Art*, 1996, volume 66, page 62

Saint Lucia's Day

In the midst of winter darkness in Sweden, the Christmas season begins on December 13, which is Saint Lucia's Day. Lucia was a young girl from Sicily who was martyred in 303 AD because of her Christian faith. Christian sailors brought the story of her kind, thoughtful life and noble death to Sweden. Over time, the Saint Lucia legend became incorporated into Swedish Christmas celebrations.

According to the old Swedish tradition, each family would choose its own Lucia, typically their eldest daughter. On this special day, the girl would rise earlier than the others and, wearing a white gown with a red sash and a wreath of candles, would serve coffee and Lucia buns to the rest of the family. This breakfast marks the beginning of several festive observances that counteract the darkness as the Christmas spirit brightens every home.

Lucia Buns

A sweet yeast bun with raisins and almonds

Buns

7 to 8 cups all-purpose flour
1 ½ cups sugar
½ teaspoon salt
2 packages active dry yeast
2 ½ cups milk
1 cup butter
½ to 1 teaspoon dried saffron
2 eggs
30 blanched almonds, chopped
2 to 4 tablespoons raisins

1. In large bowl, combine 4 cups of the flour, the sugar, salt, and yeast. In medium saucepan, combine milk, butter, and saffron. Heat until very warm (120 to 130ºF). Add to flour mixture; beat with electric mixer until well blended. Add one of the eggs; beat on medium speed 1 minute.

2. Stir in enough remaining flour, ½ cup at a time, to make dough easy to handle. Place dough on lightly floured surface. Knead dough 4 to 8 minutes or until smooth and elastic. Place dough in greased bowl. Cover bowl loosely with plastic wrap and cloth towel. Let rise in warm place (80 to 85ºF) until doubled in size, about 30 to 40 minutes.

3. Grease two large cookie sheets. Punch down dough several times to remove all air bubbles. Divide dough into thirty-six equal pieces. Roll each piece to make 10-inch rope; shape into "S." Place on cookie sheets. Cover; let rise in warm place until doubled in size, about 20 to 30 minutes.

4. Heat oven to 375ºF. Uncover dough. Beat remaining egg in small bowl. Brush tops of buns with beaten egg. Sprinkle with chopped almonds and decorate with raisins. Bake 15 to 20 minutes or until golden brown. Cool buns on wire racks.

Makes 3 dozen buns.

Tip: If you poke your finger in the dough and it leaves an impression, the dough is doubled in size. If it bounces back, it is still rising.

From *Christmas: The Annual of Christmas Literature and Art*, 1967, volume 37, page 46

Moravian Christmas *Customs*

Moravians are members of a religious group whose ancestors came from ancient Bohemia and Moravia, areas that are now part of the Czech Republic. In North America today, Moravian Church centers are in Bethlehem, Pennsylvania, and Winston-Salem, North Carolina.

At special times of the year, such as Advent and Christmas, Moravians hold a worship service called the "love feast." During the service, members share food and drink (usually a sweet bun and coffee, tea, or milk) to symbolize their devotion to each other. The tradition started in 1727, when a German count sent food to Moravians who were worshiping on his estate and did not want to leave each other for the noon meal. The gesture reminded worshipers of the early Christian "agape" meal, which was a practice associated with the Lord's Supper. Moravians continued holding love feasts on festival occasions, and they followed the tradition even after emigrating to Colonial America.

Another distinctive Moravian Christmas custom is the *putz*, a shortening of the German word *putzen* that means "to decorate" or "to clean." The Moravian *putz* is a display that depicts the story of Jesus's birth. It can be as small as a manger scene or it can fill an entire room and relate the Christmas story from Isaiah's prophecy through the flight to Egypt. Always, the manger is the center of attention.

Moravian Love Feast Buns

A sweet, buttery yeast bun

Buns

1 medium potato, peeled, cubed
¼ cup water
½ cup butter
4 to 5 cups all-purpose flour
1 cup sugar
1 teaspoon salt
1 package active dry yeast
2 eggs, beaten

Topping

¼ cup cold butter
8 teaspoons sugar

1. Place cubed potato and enough water to cover in small saucepan. Bring to a boil; reduce heat to medium-low. Cook potato until fork-tender. Drain, reserving ½ cup of the potato water. Mash potato to measure ½ cup; set aside.

2. In same saucepan, combine potato water, ¼ cup water, and ½ cup butter. Heat until very warm (120 to 130°F).

3. Meanwhile, in large bowl, combine 2 cups of the flour, the sugar, salt, and yeast; mix well. Add warm potato water mixture; beat until well blended. Add eggs and mashed potato; beat well. Add remaining flour, ½ cup at a time, beating until smooth. Cover and refrigerate 8 to 24 hours.

4. Grease cookie sheets. Punch down dough several times to remove all air bubbles. Place dough on lightly floured surface. Knead dough 6 to 10 minutes or until smooth and elastic. Divide dough into 16 equal pieces. Shape each into smooth, round bun; place on greased cookie sheets. Cover loosely with plastic wrap and cloth towel. Let rise in warm place (80 to 85°F) until doubled in size, about 45 minutes.

5. Heat oven to 375°F. Uncover dough. Cut ¼ cup cold butter into 16 equal pieces. Press one piece into center of each bun. Sprinkle each with ½ teaspoon sugar. Bake 20 to 30 minutes or until golden brown. Serve warm.

Makes 16 buns.

Tip: If you poke your finger in the dough and it leaves an impression, the dough is doubled in size. If it bounces back, it is still rising.

From *Christmas: The Annual of Christmas Literature and Art,* 1993, volume 63, page 36

Preparing for Christmas

In German Christmases past, families made traditional advent wreaths for their homes to welcome Christmas. Four weeks before Christmas, on the first Sunday in Advent, they formed evergreen branches into a circle, interlaced the branches with red ribbons, and hung them in their windows or used them as centerpieces.

In tabletop versions, families placed a red candle in the center of the wreath and four other candles in the ring around it. Each Sunday before Christmas, they would light one more candle until all four were burning on the fourth Sunday in Advent. Each day they added paper stars with Bible verses written on them. The children memorized the verses and recited them when the family gathered around the dinner table.

Germans have preserved their Christmas custom of giving thanks to God for a fruitful harvest—much like Thanksgiving services in the United States and Canada. For days before the holiday, households are busy turning out spicy cakes and cookies for Christmas callers. Germans make a cake-like bread for this occasion called Christstollen. Stollen has been traditional German fare since the Middle Ages. The shape of the long narrow cakes was said to represent the infant Jesus in the manger.

Christstollen

A lemon-glazed sweet bread with raisins

Bread

2 packages active dry yeast
3 tablespoons sugar
1 ¼ cups warm water (100 to 110°F)
5 ½ to 6 ½ cups all-purpose flour
1 cup sugar
¾ teaspoon salt
1 ½ cups butter
3 eggs
1 tablespoon vanilla or rum, if desired
1 cup raisins
1 cup slivered almonds, toasted

Glaze

1 ¼ cups powdered sugar
1 teaspoon grated lemon peel
1 to 2 tablespoons lemon juice
Milk

1. In small bowl, combine 1 package of the dry yeast and 3 tablespoons sugar. Add warm water. Stir until dissolved. Let stand 10 minutes.

2. In large bowl, combine 3 cups of the flour, 1 cup of sugar, salt, and 1 package of the dry yeast. Add yeast mixture and butter; beat with electric mixer until well blended. Add eggs and vanilla or rum, if desired; beat on medium speed 1 minute.

3. Stir in enough remaining flour, ½ cup at a time, to make dough easy to handle. Stir in raisins and almonds. Place dough on lightly floured surface. Knead dough 5 to 10 minutes or until smooth and elastic. Place dough in greased bowl. Cover bowl loosely with plastic wrap and cloth towel. Let rise in warm place (80 to 85°F) until doubled in size, about 30 to 40 minutes.

4. Grease two cookie sheets. Punch down dough several times to remove all air bubbles. Divide dough into two or three parts. Shape each part into an oval-shaped loaf; place on cookie sheet. Cover; let rise in warm place until doubled in size, about 20 to 30 minutes.

5. Heat oven to 350°F. Uncover dough. Brush loaves with melted butter. Bake 40 to 45 minutes or until golden brown. Cool on wire racks.

6. In medium bowl, mix powdered sugar, lemon peel, lemon juice, and enough milk for desired drizzling consistency. Drizzle loaves with glaze. Let stand until set.

Makes 2 or 3 loaves.

Tip: If you poke your finger in the dough and it leaves an impression, the dough is doubled in size. If it bounces back, it is still rising.

Tip: This bread freezes well. Thaw in refrigerator. Glaze just before serving.

From *Christmas: The Annual of Christmas Literature and Art*, 1973, volume 43, page 42

Czechoslovakian Custom

In days gone by, Czechoslovakian women and girls in the household used t
gather together and make their feather beds between Advent and Christma
Eve. All the while, they would tell stories about the Christ child.

Two other winter traditions tested one's fortune for the upcoming year. Unwe
young women would place a cherry tree twig in water on December 4. If i
blossomed by Christmas Eve, the one who tended it would marry during th
coming year. In another Christmas Eve custom, each person in the famil
would stick a tiny candle into a nutshell and float them all together in a pan c
water. The person whose candle remained upright the longest and burne
down the farthest was believed to have good luck in marriage and long life.

In Czechoslovakia, December 26 was considered the day of carols. Childre
would reenact pilgrimages to Bethlehem, stopping to sing at the homes of the
friends. Again on January 6, the children would reenact the magi's return t
their homes. Along the way, they would stop at each house to sing about the
journey, bless the house, and leave their initials on the door.

Vánocka

A triple-layered, braided sweet bread

Bread

4 to 4 ¼ cups all-purpose flour
½ cup sugar
1 teaspoon salt
½ teaspoon grated lemon peel
2 packages active dry yeast
1 cup milk
¼ cup water
½ cup butter
1 teaspoon vanilla
1 egg, beaten
⅓ cup chopped blanched almonds
¼ cup raisins
2 tablespoons chopped candied citron

Topping

1 egg, beaten
2 tablespoons sliced almonds
Powdered sugar

1. In large bowl, combine 2 cups of the flour, the sugar, salt, lemon peel, and yeast. In medium saucepan, combine milk, water, and butter. Heat until very warm (120 to 130°F). Add to flour mixture; beat with electric mixer until well blended. Add vanilla and one egg; beat on medium speed 1 minute.

2. Add enough remaining flour, ½ cup at a time, beating until dough is smooth, satiny, and stiff. Place dough on lightly floured surface. Knead 4 to 8 minutes or until smooth and elastic. Place dough in a bowl lightly coated with vegetable oil; turn the dough over to coat it with oil. Cover bowl loosely with plastic wrap and cloth towel. Let rise in warm place (80 to 85°F) until doubled in size.

3. Grease cookie sheet. Punch down dough several times to remove all air bubbles. Place dough on lightly floured surface. Knead in the chopped almonds, raisins, and citron. Divide dough into four equal pieces. Roll three of these pieces into 24-inch long ropes. Braid and place on greased cookie sheet. Pinch ends to seal. Divide the remaining dough piece into four smaller pieces. Roll three of these pieces into 24-inch long ropes. Braid and place on top of first braid. Pinch ends together. Cut the remaining piece of dough in half. Roll each one into a 24-inch long rope. Twist together; place on top of both of the larger braids. Tuck the ends under the larger braid. To keep twist together while rising, press three to five wooden toothpicks through twist and braids. Cover; let rise in warm place until doubled in size, about 1 hour.

4. Heat oven to 375°F. Uncover dough. Brush dough with beaten egg; sprinkle with sliced almonds. Bake 30 to 35 minutes or until deep golden brown. Sprinkle with powdered sugar.

Makes 1 loaf; 25 to 30 slices.

From *Christmas: The Annual of Christmas Literature and Art*, 1993, volume 63, page 36

Blowing of the Yule

Parts of Denmark observed an interesting custom, the "blowing in of the Yule," early in the morning of Christmas Day. At sunrise the town musicians would climb the long, steep ladders into the belfry of the church, and there—often with bitter winds sweeping over them from the North Sea—they would play four hymns, one to each corner of the compass. The first one was always "A Mighty Fortress Is Our God." The strains of music came floating down as from another world. As they finished, the church bells would begin to ring, and the "peace of Christmas" was ushered in.

Smørekringle

A flaky, pretzel-shaped pastry with almond filling

Pastry

½ cup water
2 packages active dry yeast
1 cup whipping cream
¼ cup evaporated milk
¼ cup sugar
1 teaspoon ground cardamom, if desired
3 egg yolks
3 ½ cups all-purpose flour
1 teaspoon salt
½ cup cold butter

Filling and topping

1 tube (7 ounces) almond paste (about 1 cup)
½ cup finely chopped almonds
½ cup powdered sugar
1 teaspoon almond extract
2 egg whites, divided
Coarse decorator sugar
Sliced almonds

1. In medium saucepan, heat water to 100 to 110ºF. Stir in yeast; let stand 5 minutes until dissolved. Add whipping cream, evaporated milk, sugar, cardamom, and egg yolks; blend well.

2. In large bowl, combine flour and salt. With pastry blender or two forks (or with food processor), cut in butter until mixture resembles coarse crumbs. Add yeast mixture; stir just until dry ingredients are moistened. Cover with plastic wrap. Refrigerate 12 to 24 hours.

3. While dough chills, prepare filling. Break up almond paste in medium bowl. Add chopped almonds, powdered sugar, almond extract, and one egg white; mix well until smooth. Refrigerate until assembly time.

4. After dough has chilled, place it on lightly floured surface; sprinkle with flour. Roll dough to a 24-inch square. Fold dough into thirds to make long, narrow strip. Roll again until it is 36 inches long and about ¼-inch thick. Spread almond mixture over dough to within 1 inch of each end. Starting on one long side, roll up dough. Beat remaining egg white in small bowl; brush over all sides of dough. Roll in coarse sugar.

5. Line cookie sheet with parchment paper or grease and flour cookie sheet. Arrange dough on cookie sheet in the shape of a large pretzel. Cover with plastic wrap and cloth towel. Let rise in warm place (80 to 85ºF) for 45 minutes. (Dough will not double in size.)

6. Heat oven to 375ºF. Uncover dough. Brush again with egg white; sprinkle with sliced almonds. Bake 25 to 30 minutes or until golden brown.

Makes 1 loaf.

From *Christmas: The Annual of Christmas Literature and Art*, 1993, volume 63, page 38

Sharing in the Christmas Fortune

Candles and cake are important in the traditional Hungarian celebration of Christmas. Three candles would be placed in the hollow of a coffee cake ring. The first would be lit on Christmas Eve. The father in the home would make the sign of the cross, saying, "Christ is born," to which the family would respond, "He is born indeed." The second would be lit at noon on Christmas Day. The father would run out to the barn and put the warm candle in the grain. By the number of grains adhering to it, he would foretell what his crops would be like for the year. The third candle would be lit on New Year's Day. The cake would be cut on the sixth of January. Each member of the family would get a slice to symbolize his or her share in the good fortune of the coming year.

Mâkos és Diós Kalács

A sweet bread with poppy seed filling

Bread

5 to 5 ¼ cups all-purpose flour
½ cup sugar
1 ½ teaspoons salt
2 packages active dry yeast
¾ cup milk
½ cup water
⅔ cup butter
3 eggs

Filling and glaze

1 ½ cups poppy seeds
1 ½ cups chopped walnuts
1 cup sugar
½ cup light or dark raisins
2 teaspoons grated lemon peel
1 can (12 ounces) evaporated milk
1 egg, beaten

1. In large bowl, combine 3 cups of the flour, ½ cup sugar, the salt, and yeast. In medium saucepan, combine milk, water, and butter. Heat until very warm (120 to 130°F). Add to flour mixture; beat with electric mixer until well blended. Add three eggs; beat on medium speed 1 minute.

2. Add enough remaining flour, ½ cup at a time, beating until dough is smooth and soft. Divide dough into three pieces; place in three greased bowls. Cover each bowl with plastic wrap and cloth towel. Let rise in warm place (80 to 85°F) until doubled in size, about 1 hour.

3. Meanwhile, mix poppy seeds and walnuts in blender container; blend until ground. In medium saucepan, combine 1 cup sugar, raisins, lemon peel, and evaporated milk. Cook over medium-low heat, stirring constantly, until sugar is dissolved. Stir in ground poppy seed mixture. Bring to a boil; boil 1 minute, stirring constantly. Cool completely.

4. Grease three cookie sheets. Lightly oil 30-inch square on counter or work surface. For each loaf, place dough from one bowl on surface; do not punch down dough. Sprinkle dough with flour; roll to 24 x 12-inch rectangle. Spoon ⅓ of poppy seed mixture on top and spread to within 2 inches of one long edge. Starting with filling-covered long edge, roll up dough; shape into ring, and place on greased cookie sheet. Repeat with other two portions of dough. Brush each loaf with beaten egg. Cover loaves; let rise in warm place until doubled in size, about 30 minutes.

5. Heat oven to 325°F. Uncover dough. Brush each loaf again with beaten egg. Bake 30 to 45 minutes or until light golden brown. Cool on wire racks.

Makes 3 loaves.

Tip: If you poke your finger in the dough and it leaves an impression, the dough is doubled in size. If it bounces back, it is still rising.

Tip: Poppy seeds may be purchased in bulk at food cooperatives or health/specialty stores.

From *Christmas: The Annual of Christmas Literature and Art*, 1993, volume 63, page 37

Preparing for Christmas

In Christmases past, Finnish people would strive to finish all work by noon on the day before Christmas. Families would wash the whole house. In some regions, people brought in straw or evergreen boughs to cover the floor. The children slept on these floor coverings on Christmas Eve to commemorate the birthplace of the Christ child.

Finnish families also made Christmas decorations from readily available materials. For example, they shaped moist bread dough into a circle to represent a wreath and let it dry. When the dough was ready, they painted their wreath a variety of bright colors. They made swags from straw and colored paper to drape around the Christmas tree. They also hung cut-out sugar cookies on the tree by making loops out of frosting, drying the loops, then cementing them onto the cookies using moist frosting. When the frosting cement dried, they strung thread through the loops and tied the cookies to the tree.

Coffee Braids

A sweet bread with cardamom

Bread

4 to 5 cups all-purpose flour
½ cup sugar
½ teaspoon salt
3 to 4 cardamom seeds, ground
1 package active dry yeast
½ cup very warm milk (120 to 130°F)
¼ cup butter, melted
3 eggs

1. In large bowl, combine 2 cups of the flour, the sugar, salt, cardamom, and yeast. Add warm milk, melted butter, and eggs. Beat with electric mixer on low speed 1 minute, scraping bowl frequently. Beat on medium speed 1 minute.

2. Stir in enough remaining flour, ½ cup at a time, to make dough easy to handle. Place dough on lightly floured surface. Knead dough 5 to 10 minutes or until smooth and elastic. Place dough in greased bowl. Cover bowl loosely with plastic wrap and cloth towel. Let rise in warm place (80 to 85°F) until doubled in size, about 30 to 40 minutes.

3. Grease large cookie sheet. Punch down dough several times to remove all air bubbles. Divide dough in half; divide each half into three equal parts. Roll each part into 14-inch rope. For each coffee cake, braid three ropes together; seal ends. Place on cookie sheet. Cover; let rise in warm place until doubled in size, about 30 to 40 minutes.

4. Heat oven to 375°F. Uncover dough. Bake 25 to 30 minutes or until golden brown. Cool loaves on wire racks.

Makes 2 loaves.

Tip: If you poke your finger in the dough and it leaves an impression, the dough is doubled in size. If it bounces back, it is still rising.

From *Christmas: The Annual of Christmas Literature and Art*, 1957, volume 27, page 29

Saint Barbara's Grain and the *Yule Log*

In the Provence region of France, the Christmas season was traditionally started with the planting of Saint Barbara's grain on December 4. Farmers put wheat grains on two or three plates, added water, and placed the plates in the warm ashes of the fireplace or on a sunny windowsill. If the grains sprouted well, families believed there would be a plentiful harvest next year.

The Yule log was known as *cacho-fiò*. The log was taken from a fruit-bearing tree, usually an almond or an olive tree. Olive trees were considered especially sacred; it was believed lightning never strikes them. In the Alps region, French people cut logs from oak trees. Customarily, the whole family had to take part in bringing the *cacho-fiò* in—the grandfather, father, or son would cut it and the rest would help to carry it home. The log was brought into the house with the hands of the youngest and oldest family members touching it. After placing in on the hearth, the family poured three libations of boiled wine over the *cacho-fiò*, the last one in the name of the Trinity. Then the family filled the cup once more, this time to pass, hand to hand and lip to lip, from the youngest to the oldest member of the family circle.

Birewecke

A dried-fruit-and-nut bread, resembling fruitcake

Fruit Mixture

1 package (6 ounces) mixed dried fruit bits
1 cup dried apples or pears
1 cup pitted prunes
2 cups water
1 cup dried, pitted figs, coarsely chopped
1 cup mixed candied fruits
1 cup light or dark raisins
$\frac{1}{2}$ cup brandy, sherry, or kirsch
2 cups chopped walnuts
1 cup slivered or sliced almonds
1 cup sugar
$\frac{1}{4}$ cup ground cinnamon

Bread

3 cups all-purpose flour
1 teaspoon salt
Dash sugar
1 package active dry yeast
$\frac{1}{2}$ cup water
$\frac{1}{2}$ cup butter
3 eggs

Glaze

$\frac{1}{2}$ cup light corn syrup
Walnut halves, toasted

1. In medium saucepan, combine fruit bits, dried apples or pears, prunes, and water. Bring to a boil; cook 20 minutes over medium-low heat until fruit is tender, stirring occasionally. Cut whole fruits into smaller pieces. Spoon into nonmetal bowl. Add figs, candied fruits, raisins, and brandy. Cover; let stand 8 hours or overnight. Stir in walnuts, almonds, 1 cup sugar, and cinnamon.

2. In large bowl, combine 2 cups of the flour, the salt, dash sugar, and yeast. In medium saucepan, combine water and butter. Heat until very warm (120 to 130ºF). Add to flour mixture; beat with electric mixer until well blended. Add eggs; beat on medium speed 1 minute. Add remaining flour, $\frac{1}{2}$ cup at a time, beating until dough is smooth and soft. Let stand 15 minutes.

3. Grease three (8 x 4-inch) loaf pans. Stir fruit mixture into dough until well blended. Divide dough into three portions. Place one portion in each greased pan. Cover pans with plastic wrap and cloth towel. Let rise in warm place (80 to 85ºF) until dough almost fills the pans, about 3 hours. (Dough is heavy and rises slowly.)

4. Heat oven to 375ºF. Uncover dough. Bake 45 to 50 minutes or until golden brown and firm to touch when tapped in center. Carefully remove loaves from pans; cool completely on wire racks. Wrap loaves in plastic wrap. Place in cool, dry place or freeze; age at least one week.

5. Prepare glaze. If bread was frozen, thaw completely. In small saucepan, heat corn syrup to boiling. Brush over tops of loaves. Arrange walnut halves over each loaf; brush with corn syrup again. Let stand until set.

Makes 3 loaves.

From *Christmas: The Annual of Christmas Literature and Art*, 1993, volume 63, page 37

Three Kings Day

Anchoring the end of the Christmas season, Three Kings Day, January 6, is widely celebrated in Mexico. The customs are rooted in the biblical account of the day the magi brought gifts of gold, frankincense, and myrrh to the young Christ child.

Centuries ago, Spanish missionaries to Mexico used nativity scenes and masses as means of teaching native peoples about Christianity. Each night after the religious ceremony, they praised the Christ child in song, offered prayers, and distributed sweets. From these ceremonies, the custom of giving presents emerged. On the night of January 5, children would set out their shoes before going to bed in hopes of a visit from the magi. They would also leave gifts for the camels, such as bundles of hay or freshly cut grasses.

Rosca de Reyes, or Three Kings Bread, would traditionally be served on January 6. Families would sometimes hide a small doll (representing Baby Jesus) or a coin wrapped in foil in the cake. Each person would cut his or her own slice. The one who found the "prize" would be nominated to hold a party on or before February 2, which is Candlemas. The party would mark the end of the Christmas season.

Rosca de Reyes

"Three Kings Bread"—cake-like bread with icing

Bread

4 cups all-purpose flour
½ cup sugar
1 ½ teaspoons salt
2 packages active dry yeast
⅔ cup milk
¼ cup water
⅓ cup lard, shortening, butter, or margarine
3 eggs, beaten
2 cups mixed candied fruit and/or raisins

Icing

1 cup powdered sugar
2 to 3 tablespoons milk or water
Candied fruit and nuts

Special equipment

Ring molds
Tiny china dolls or foil-wrapped coins (if desired)

1. In large bowl, combine 2 cups of the flour, sugar, salt, and yeast. In medium saucepan, combine milk, water, and lard. Heat until very warm (120 to 130ºF). Add to flour mixture; beat with electric mixer until well blended. Add eggs; beat 1 minute or until smooth and satiny.

2. Add remaining flour, ½ cup at a time, beating until dough is smooth and stiff. Stir in candied fruit. Cover bowl with plastic wrap and cloth towel. Let rise in warm place (80 to 85ºF) until doubled in size, about 1 to 2 hours. (Bread will rise slowly.)

3. Grease two (8-inch) ring molds. Divide dough in half. On lightly floured surface, shape each half into 20-inch long log. Place each in greased ring mold. If desired, tuck clean tiny china dolls or foil-wrapped coins into each loaf, covering with dough so they don't show. Cover loaves; let rise in warm place until doubled in size, about 1 to 2 hours.

4. Heat oven to 375ºF. Uncover dough. Bake 25 to 30 minutes or until golden brown and toothpick inserted in center comes out clean. Cool slightly. Remove from pans; cool on wire racks.

5. In medium bowl, mix powdered sugar and enough milk for desired drizzling consistency. Drizzle mixture over top of cooled loaves. Decorate with candied fruit and nuts as desired. Let stand until set. (Be sure to let guests and family know if the bread contains inedible items, so they can be careful.)

Makes 2 rings.

Tip: If you poke your finger in the dough and it leaves an impression, the dough is doubled in size. If it bounces back, it is still rising.

From *Christmas: The Annual of Christmas Literature and Art*, 1993, volume 63, page 39

The Praesepio

Italian Christmas celebrations customarily would start with the *novena*, or nine days of prayers. On the first day, each family would set up a manger scene, called a *praesepio*, in their home. This tradition dates back to the 13th century. The scene would usually be set up on the bottom shelf of a pyramid-shaped display, called a *ceppo;* it would be gaily decorated with pinecones, candles, and colorful paper. The *ceppo* would even take the place of a Christmas tree. Every morning, the family would gather around the manger scene for prayers.

The first *praesepio* figures were simply carved from wood or modeled in wax or clay. Over time they became increasingly elaborate. In addition to the holy family, shepherds with sheep or dogs and angel messengers were added. Then came the magi, often richly dressed, with their retinue of servants and camels. Over the years other figures became common: Italian villagers thronging to the manger or working at their trades—baking, fishing, farming, or building. Whole castles or towns and the surrounding countryside are part of many *praesepio* today. The tiny hand-carved or cast nativity figures are often passed down through generations of family members.

Petele

A fried yeast bread

Bread

3 ½ cups all-purpose flour
1 teaspoon salt
1 package active dry yeast
1 cup very warm water (120 to 130°F)
Oil for deep-frying

Topping

Salt or sugar, if desired

1. In large bowl, combine 2 cups of the flour, 1 teaspoon salt, and yeast. Add warm water. Beat with electric mixer on low speed 1 minute, scraping bowl frequently.

2. Stir in enough remaining flour, ¼ cup at a time, until dough is easy to handle. Place dough on lightly floured surface. Knead dough 5 to 10 minutes or until smooth and elastic. Place dough in greased bowl. Cover bowl loosely with plastic wrap and cloth towel. Let rise in warm place (80 to 85°F) until doubled in size, about 40 to 60 minutes.

3. Heat 2 to 3 inches oil in large deep skillet or deep fryer to 350°F. Break off pieces of dough and shape into strips 6-inches long and 1- to 1 ½-inches wide. If desired, shape into circle like a doughnut. Drop three or four petele into hot oil at a time. Cook until golden brown, turning once with fork. Drain on paper towels. If desired, sprinkle rolls with salt or sugar while still warm.

Makes about 2 dozen rolls.

Tip: If you poke your finger in the dough and it leaves an impression, the dough is doubled in size. If it bounces back, it is still rising.

From *Christmas: The Annual of Christmas Literature and Art*, 1978, volume 48, page 18

Las Posadas

In Mexico *Las Posadas* begins on December 16. A *posada* is a resting place or lodge; the *Las Posadas* celebrations commemorate Mary and Joseph's search for lodging in Bethlehem. Traditionally for nine days, people would hold pageants of the holy family winding along the streets, searching for a place to stay. Occasionally there would be a religious drama on stage.

More often, the *posadas* would be celebrated by people attending parties in each other's homes. After a procession to the house, partygoers would sing a litany outside. Often guests would be divided into two groups: the cruel innkeepers and the pilgrims who would beg for shelter. When one kindhearted innkeeper would invite the wayfarers to enter, they would pray, sing sacred songs, and proceed to an altar decorated with tinsel and flowers. A lullaby would follow while someone placed an image of the Christ child in the manger.

In Mexican town plazas on Christmas Eve, street vendors would sell *bunuelos*, a holiday treat. The sweet frybread would be served on cracked or chipped pottery plates, which, after the *bunuelos* were eaten, would be broken by throwing them on the ground. This tradition may be remnant of ancient Indian ceremonies in which the broken pottery symbolized the end of the old year.

Bunuelos

A slightly sweet, fried bread

Bread

4 cups all-purpose flour
2 tablespoons sugar
3 teaspoons baking powder
1/4 cup vegetable oil
2 tablespoons milk
2 eggs, beaten
1 cup warm water
1 cup vegetable oil for frying

Topping

1/2 cup sugar
3 tablespoons ground cinnamon

1. In large bowl, combine flour, 2 tablespoons sugar, and baking powder. Add the 1/4 cup oil, milk, and eggs; blend well. Add water; mix until dough is smooth. (If dough is dry, add additional water, 1 teaspoon at a time, until smooth.)

2. Place dough on a lightly floured surface. Knead dough 3 to 5 minutes or until smooth. Divide dough into twenty to twenty-four pieces; shape each piece into a 1 1/2- to 2-inch ball. Flatten each ball into a round shape with the palm of your hand. Cover with cloth towel; let stand 20 minutes.

3. One at a time, place rounds on a lightly floured surface. Using a rolling pin, roll out the dough to a 6- to 7-inch circle. Let them stand 5 minutes.

4. Heat 1 cup oil in large deep skillet or deep fryer to 360ºF. One at a time, drop dough rounds into oil. Cook until golden brown and crisp, turning once. Drain on paper towels. In small bowl, combine 1/2 cup sugar and cinnamon. Sprinkle hot bunuelos with sugar mixture.

Makes 1 1/2 to 2 dozen bunuelos.

From *Christmas: The Annual of Christmas Literature and Art*, 1991, volume 61, page 26

Norwegian Christmas *Treats*

In some Norwegian homes, the first Christmas celebration is December 23, *Lille Julaften* (Little Christmas Eve). This supper previews the special foods that have been accumulating during holiday preparations. Sometimes a small but unique gift waits at the plate of each family member and guest, placed there, of course by *Julenisse*, the Norwegian version of Santa Claus.

Pre-breakfast treats are part of the Christmas Day celebration. Before the children and guests are up, parents go around to each bedroom, serving hot chocolate or currant juice, lefse, and cookies to everyone in the house on Christmas morning. It is an especially looked-forward-to delight.

Lefse

A thin, soft, potato flatbread

Bread

6 medium russet potatoes
½ cup butter
½ cup half-and-half
1 tablespoon salt
½ to 1 cup all-purpose flour

Topping

Butter
Brown sugar or white sugar, if desired

Special equipment

Potato ricer
Lefse grill (optional)
Lefse stick (optional)

1. Place potatoes in large Dutch oven; cover with water. Bring to a boil. Reduce heat to medium; cook potatoes until fork-tender. Cool slightly.

2. Remove skins from potatoes. Press potatoes through potato ricer into large bowl. (There should be about 6 cups.) Add butter, half-and-half, and salt; mix well. Stir in flour, 1 tablespoon at a time, until mixture is smooth and of rolling consistency.

3. On lightly floured surface, roll generous tablespoonfuls of dough into very thin rounds. Heat griddle or nonstick skillet over medium-high heat (or use lefse grill). Cook each round on both sides just until brown spots begin to appear. (If available, use lefse stick to turn the lefse and remove it from heat.) Cool between towels.

4. If desired, spread with butter and brown or white sugar. Cut into pie-shaped sections and fold or roll up.

Makes 2 ½ to 3 ½ dozen lefse rounds.

From *Christmas: The Annual of Christmas Literature and Art*, 1963, volume 33, page 64

Candles and Carolers

One old Irish tradition was to place a candle in the front window of each home to illuminate the way for the holy family. On Christmas Eve, the youngest child (preferably a young girl named Mary) would stand at the hearth holding a small pine branch. At the moment the Christmas bell rang, she would take a flame from the fire in the hearth and carry it to the candle.

On the day after Christmas Day, Irish revelry would heat up for the feast of Saint Stephen, with the Wren Boys' march. Young men would hunt down a wren and then march from house to house singing a special song for the day: "The wren, the wren, the king of all birds / Saint Stephen's day was caught in the furze; / Although he is little, his family is great, / So rise up, landlady, and give us a treat."

The Wren Boys' tradition reaches back to a time following the Danish invasion of Ireland. One day, the Irish found the Danes asleep. Their drummer boy had finished eating and dozed off, when a wren spotted crumbs on the drumhead and alighted to eat them up. Alarmed by the tapping, the boy woke up, spotted the Irish, and began pounding his drum to awaken the Danes, who then defeated the Irish troops. Thus, young Irishmen used to hunt a wren on Christmas Day to avenge the bird's betrayal.

Scones

Sweet bread to serve with coffee or tea or as sandwiches

Bread

2 ½ cups all-purpose flour
2 tablespoons sugar
3 teaspoons baking powder
½ teaspoon salt
½ cup slightly softened butter, cut into small pieces
⅔ cup milk

Topping suggestions

Jam
Thinly sliced smoked turkey or cooked ham
Cranberry sauce or fruit chutney

1. Heat oven to 425°F. In large bowl, combine flour, sugar, baking powder, and salt. With pastry blender or two forks, cut in butter until mixture resembles fine crumbs. With fork, stir in milk until soft dough forms.

2. Shape dough into ball; place on lightly floured surface. Knead dough ten to twelve times or until smooth. Roll dough to ½-inch thickness. Cut with 2-inch round cutter, rerolling dough as necessary. Place scones on ungreased cookie sheet with sides touching.

3. Bake 12 to 16 minutes or until golden brown. Remove from cookie sheet; cool on wire racks. Serve scones with jam or make turkey or ham sandwiches with, if desired, cranberry sauce or fruit chutney.

Makes about 1 ½ dozen scones.

From *Christmas: The Annual of Christmas Literature and Art*, 1992, volume 62, page 55

Dipping Day

The custom of "Dipping Day" was unique to Sweden, stemming from a famine many Christmas Eves ago when the only food available was black bread and thin broth. According to the tradition that emerged afterward, at noon on Christmas Eve day, everyone would gather in the kitchen for *doppa i grytan*, meaning "dip-in-the-pot." The Christmas *korv*, or sausages, would simmer in a large kettle on the stove. Each person would solemnly dip a slice of dark rye bread called *vörtlimpor* into the kettle of steaming broth and eat it to ensure good luck in the coming year.

Even today, the Swedish household specializes in fancy breads for Christmas—saffron bread, fennel bread, caraway bread, and *vörtlimpor*. Traditionally, one loaf would be shaped like a boar's head, decorated, and allowed to remain on the dining room table throughout the holiday as a prayer for next year's harvest.

Vörtlimpor

A dark rye bread

Bread

4 cups dark rye flour
½ cup chopped candied orange peel
2 tablespoons grated fresh orange peel
2 tablespoons crushed anise or fennel seed
1 tablespoon sugar
1 teaspoon salt
2 packages active dry yeast
1 bottle (12 ounces) dark stout beer
1 cup water
¾ cup dark molasses
3 tablespoons lard or butter
2 cups bread flour

Glaze

2 tablespoons dark molasses
2 tablespoons water

1. In large bowl, combine rye flour, candied orange peel, fresh orange peel, anise (or fennel), sugar, salt, and yeast. In medium saucepan, combine beer, 1 cup water, ¾ cup dark molasses, and lard. Heat until very warm (120 to 130ºF). Add to flour mixture; beat with electric mixer until smooth and firm.

2. Add bread flour; beat 1 minute or until dough is stiff and smooth. Cover bowl with plastic wrap and cloth towel. Let rise in warm place (80 to 85ºF) until doubled in size, about 1 hour.

3. Grease cookie sheet. Uncover dough. Punch down dough several times to remove all air bubbles. Pinch off enough dough to make two (3-inch) balls; set aside. On lightly floured surface, shape remaining dough into a large smooth ball. Place on greased cookie sheet; flatten large ball to 10-inch round. Roll each of the smaller dough balls into 15-inch long rope. With a sharp knife, cut a 5-inch long slash into each end of each rope. Cross ropes on center of larger loaf; curl slashed sections away from center of each rope to form a flower-like design. (Do not press down.) Cover; let rise in warm place until almost doubled in size, about 1 hour.

4. Heat oven to 350ºF. Uncover dough. Bake 35 to 45 minutes or until skewer inserted in center of loaf comes out clean. About halfway through baking, mix together 2 tablespoons molasses and 2 tablespoons water. Brush mixture over partially baked loaf. Remove from oven; brush with glaze again. Cool on wire rack.

Makes 1 loaf.

From *Christmas: The Annual of Christmas Literature and Art*, 1993, volume 63, page 38

Scottish Christmas Customs

In Scotland, traditionalists have many interesting beliefs. The celebration of Christmas was said to be favored by a waxing moon. No home would leave a piece of work unfinished during this season. On Christmas Eve everyone in the household would stay up until midnight, because "open house" was held for all wayfarers. In remembrance of the Christ child whowandered through fields and towns on this night, no visitor would be turned away without being served. Foods would include shortbread, fruitcake, oat cakes, Scotch eggs, and cheese; a slice of Christmas cheese was said to have magical virtues. The fire would not be allowed to go out on this night. If it did, wicked elves would come down the chimney to dance in the ashes!

Scotch Eggs

A traditional, savory British tidbit

Ingredients

1 ½ pounds bulk pork sausage
1 uncooked egg
6 hard-cooked eggs
¼ to ½ cup dry bread crumbs
Spicy mustard, if desired

1. Heat oven to 375ºF. In large bowl, combine sausage and uncooked egg; mix well. Divide mixture into six equal portions. Remove shells from hard-cooked eggs. Mold each portion of sausage mixture around a hard-cooked egg. Roll sausage-covered eggs in bread crumbs. Place on rack in shallow baking pan.

2. Bake 45 to 60 minutes or until sausage is thoroughly cooked. To serve, cut each egg into three or four slices. If desired, serve with spicy mustard.

Makes 1 ½ to 2 dozen appetizers.

From *Christmas: The Annual of Christmas Literature and Art*, 1992, volume 62, page 55

Waits and Wassailers

In some regions, English carolers were sometimes called "waits." The term "waits" may have come from the watchmen of former centuries, who joined together at Christmastime, singing at various households while making their rounds. Led by a "shouter," the waits carried musical instruments and often collected funds to be used for a party on the eve of Epiphany, or Twelfth Night.

The tradition of wassailing seems to have arisen with the Danes when they briefly ruled England. The word "wassail" derives from the Saxon phrase of *waes hael*, meaning "to be in good health" and "to be fortunate." Either on New Year's Eve or Twelfth Night, farmers would "wassail" their apple trees by drinking a toast of cider and shooting guns into the bare branches. This was done to assure a good harvest. In West Country, farmers gathered on Twelfth Night to eat hot cakes soaked in cider. While some partygoers banged on pots and shot into the apple trees, other guests joyfully sang wassail songs and drank cider. In some rural districts the wassailing parties were called "apple-howling." In northern England, wassailers carried wooden bowls on their heads and, singing old rhymes or traditional carols, went from house to house.

Mushroom Tarts

Bite-sized treats perfect for tea or as an appetizer

Pastry

1/2 cup butter or margarine, softened
1 package (3 ounces) cream cheese, softened
1 cup all-purpose flour
1/4 teaspoon salt

Filling

1/4 cup butter or margarine
2 tablespoons vegetable oil
8 ounces mushrooms, finely chopped
1/4 cup finely chopped fresh parsley
2 tablespoons finely chopped green onions
1/2 cup freshly grated Parmesan cheese
1/3 cup dry bread crumbs
1 1/2 teaspoons finely chopped fresh or 1 teaspoon dried marjoram
1/4 teaspoon salt
1/8 teaspoon pepper

1. In medium bowl, mix 1/2 cup butter and cream cheese until smooth. Add flour and salt; mix well. Wrap pastry tightly with plastic wrap and refrigerate 1 hour for easier handling.

2. Heat oven to 350ºF. Divide pastry into twenty-four (1-inch) balls. Place each ball in ungreased miniature muffin cup or tiny tart pan; press over bottom and up sides to form cups. Refrigerate while making filling.

3. In large skillet, heat 1/4 cup butter and the oil over medium-high heat until melted and hot. Add mushrooms, parsley, and onions; cook and stir about 5 minutes or until tender. Remove from heat. Stir in all remaining ingredients. Cool 1 hour.

4. Spoon filling into pastry-filled muffin cups. Bake 15 to 20 minutes or until filling bubbles and pastry is light golden brown.

Makes 2 dozen tarts.

Tip: Filled-but-unbaked tarts can be frozen and baked at a later date. To bake after freezing, let stand about 1 hour at room temperature or until thawed. Bake at 350ºF for 20 to 25 minutes.

From *Christmas: The Annual of Christmas Literature and Art*, 1992, volume 62, page 53

Father Christmas & the English Yule Log

English children hang stockings for Father Christmas to fill with toys. An old custom was for young children to write up a wish list of presents and throw the list into the hearth. If the paper was sucked up the chimney, the child believed he or she would receive the requested presents. But if the paper burned, the child would either need to write another list or worry that he or she would not be rewarded!

The Yule log tradition in Britain survives from pagan antiquity, deriving from 11th-century Scandinavian invaders to the isles. As part of the enormous bonfires during winter solstice, the Yule log later evolved during feudal and medieval times to become a traditional source of light and warmth in the home. Prior to Christmas, it was dragged into the house, festooned with ribbons, in triumphal processions—a good omen to all who participated. Bringing in the Yule log signaled a time to bury the hatchet, to forgive one's enemies, to patch up quarrels, and to join hands at the wassail bowl. The log was supposed to be kept burning through all twelve days of Christmas, then stored inside so that the charred remains would protect the home from fire, lightning, and evil spirits. The following year the embers were rekindled to light a new log. Today the Yule Log tradition survives through the shape of cakes and decorations, rather than as actual timbers.

Potted Shrimp

A spread for crackers or cucumber slices, or a stuffing for tomatoes

Ingredients

8 ounces uncooked large shrimp, peeled and deveined
2 cloves garlic, minced
½ cup dry sherry
6 tablespoons butter or margarine
Salt and white pepper to taste

1. In medium saucepan, combine shrimp, garlic, sherry, and butter. Cook over medium-high heat about 5 minutes, until shrimp are firm and pink, stirring frequently. Add salt and white pepper to taste.

2. Spoon mixture into food processor bowl or blender. Process until puréed. Spoon into serving dish. Cover with plastic wrap and refrigerate 1 to 2 hours or until mixture is chilled and set. Store in refrigerator no longer than 3 days.

Makes about 1 cup.

Tip: Cooked shrimp may be used instead of uncooked shrimp. Before adding the shrimp, cook garlic, sherry, and butter just until butter is melted and the mixture is well blended. Then stir in the cooked shrimp.

From *Christmas: The Annual of Christmas Literature and Art*, 1992, volume 62, page 53

Danish Tree Traditions

In Denmark, the Christmas tree has been the center of many traditions. On Christmas Eve, when the festive dinner was over, the parents would leave the room to decorate the tree with candles. The lighted candles—"living light"—symbolized the Christmas spirit, which filled the hearts of the faithful with peace and joy. Other decorations included Danish flags, straw figures, heart-shaped ornaments, and stars. When the parents finished, the doors were opened, revealing to the children the gleaming Christmas tree in all its splendor.

According to custom, the youngest child would enter the room first, and soon the whole family gathered in a circle around the tree to sing carols to the one who is the light of the world. One hymn sung in Danish homes throughout generations was "The Happy Christmas Comes Once More." This hymn by N. F. S. Grundtvig, a prolific hymn writer, contains a stanza that picks up the theme of light:

O holy Child, thy manger gleams
Till earth and heaven glow with its beams,
Till midnight noon's broad light hath won,
And Jacob's star outshines the sun.

Stegt Julegass

A traditional goose for the Christmas feast

Ingredients

1 (10- to 12-pound) fresh or frozen goose, thawed
1 teaspoon salt
3 to 4 medium apples, peeled, quartered
2 cups pitted prunes, chopped
2 tablespoons all-purpose flour

1. Heat oven to 450ºF. Remove giblets, neck, and excess fat from inside of goose; rub cavity with ½ teaspoon of the salt. Stuff goose with apples and prunes. Close cavity with metal skewers or sew shut with string. Tuck wing tips under; secure legs with string. Place goose on rack in shallow roasting pan, breast side up.

2. Bake 45 minutes. Remove roaster from oven; drain and discard accumulated fat from pan. Sprinkle goose with remaining ½ teaspoon salt and the flour. Reduce oven temperature to 350ºF.

3. Bake 2 to 2 ½ hours or until meat thermometer inserted into meaty portion of thigh reaches 180 to 185ºF. During baking, continue to remove excess fat as it accumulates in the pan. Tent loosely with foil if goose becomes too brown. When done, remove from oven; cover and let stand 20 to 30 minutes before carving.

Makes 8 servings.

Tip: Remove the fat from the pan as the goose cooks to keep the grease from spattering in the oven.

From *Christmas: The Annual of Christmas Literature and Art*, 1977, volume 47, page 48

Kučios

Christmas is called *Kučios* in Lithuania. Traditionally, December 24 was considered the most sacred day. Only work connected with preparation for the feast itself was allowed. Mending clothing or chopping wood on Christmas Eve was believed to be an ill omen for both people and their farm animals. The household fasted all day until the first evening star appeared. Then the family would sit down to a meal where an empty place was left for relatives who could not be present or had passed away. Under the tablecloth, the family would place a bed of straw or hay to symbolize the birth of Christ in a stable. That same evening the farm animals would receive their own special kucia— an ample measure of hay, oats, and other grains.

As in other countries, traditions in Lithuania illustrate a mix of religious belief and superstition. At midnight animals were thought to kneel and pray or even speak. If anyone intentionally listened, he or she would die within the year, so the belief goes. It was also believed that at midnight, water in wells would turn to wine, bees in their hives would predict the future, and sheep by their behavior could signal bad or good omens for the coming year.

Mesos Viritinioi

Delicious beef dumplings

Filling

1 pound lean ground beef
$\frac{1}{2}$ cup finely chopped onion
$\frac{1}{4}$ teaspoon salt
$\frac{1}{8}$ teaspoon pepper
$\frac{1}{3}$ cup beef broth

Dough

2 eggs
3 $\frac{1}{2}$ to 4 cups all-purpose flour
1 cup water

1. In medium bowl, combine ground beef, onion, salt, pepper, and beef broth. Shape into $\frac{1}{2}$- to $\frac{3}{4}$-inch meatballs.

2. Beat eggs in large bowl. Add water, then slowly blend in flour, $\frac{1}{2}$ cup at a time. Mix until soft dough forms. Knead with hands. Divide dough into three or four parts for easier handling. Place dough on floured surface. Roll to $\frac{1}{8}$-inch thickness. With 2-inch round cutter or rim of drinking glass dipped in flour, cut rounds from dough.

3. For each dumpling, place meatball in center of dough round. Fold dough over; press edges with fork to seal.

4. In large saucepan, bring salted water to a boil. Drop meat dumplings in water. Boil 8 to 10 minutes or until firm. Serve warm.

Makes 10 to 11 dozen meat dumplings.

From *Christmas: The Annual of Christmas Literature and Art*, 1957, volume 27, page 31

Christmas Spirituals

The African-American spiritual "Go Tell It on the Mountain" emerged in the United States during the slave era. Like most spirituals, the song cannot be traced to one person alone. Slaves created these songs in the fields where they worked or in their cabins, and they passed the spirituals on as oral tradition. Most song lyrics were inspired by Old Testament stories, especially those passages that speak of the Hebrews in bondage. Likewise, some spirituals draw from New Testament passages that record Jesus's suffering and death. "Go Tell It on the Mountain" is one of the few that relate the story of Jesus's birth. The familiar refrain goes:

Go tell it on the mountain,
Over the hills and everywhere;
Go tell it on the mountain
That Jesus Christ is born.

John Wesley Work Jr., born in 1871, was a professor at Fisk University in Nashville. He led the effort to preserve, study, and perform spirituals. In the process of recording "Go Tell It on the Mountain," he wrote these verses:

When I was a seeker
I sought both night and day,
I asked the Lord to help me,
And he showed me the way.

He made me a watchman
Upon a city wall,
And if I am a Christian,
I am the least of all.

Angel Honey Cake with Almonds

A sweet, rich cake

Cake

4 eggs
1 cup sugar
1 cup honey
¼ cup vegetable oil
1 tablespoon instant coffee granules or crystals
½ cup boiling water
3 cups all-purpose flour
1 ½ teaspoons baking powder
½ teaspoon baking soda
¼ teaspoon ground cinnamon
1 cup chopped almonds
2 to 3 teaspoons grated orange peel (peel from 1 orange)

1. Heat oven to 325°F. Grease 9 x 13 x 2-inch pan. Line pan with wax paper. Beat eggs in large bowl until frothy. Add sugar; beat 30 seconds. Add honey and oil; beat 30 seconds.

2. In small bowl, mix coffee granules and boiling water; stir until dissolved. Add to sugar mixture. Add flour, baking powder, baking soda, and cinnamon; blend well. Stir in almonds and orange peel. Spoon and spread in lined pan.

3. Bake 40 to 50 minutes or until toothpick inserted in center comes out clean. Cool slightly. Invert cake on wire rack; cool completely.

Makes 1 cake, 12 to 16 servings.

From *Christmas: The Annual of Christmas Literature and Art*, 1997, volume 67, page 63

The First Decorated Christmas Cards

Englishman Sir Henry Cole was busier than usual just before Christmas 1846. In other years he had written Christmas letters to relatives and friends, but this year he realized he would not have time. He decided to have a Christmas card designed, so that he might send one to all his relatives and friends. So began a tradition.

Cole commissioned an artist-friend from the Royal Academy, John Calcott Housley, to carry out the idea. Housley designed a three-paneled card with a trellis entwined with a grapevine. The largest panel showed a family Christmas party. The panels on either side depicted two of the oldest Christmas customs—feeding the hungry and clothing the needy. The words of the greeting have lasted through the years: "A Merry Christmas and a Happy New Year to you."

During the next few years, Christmas cards were printed as orders for individuals; they were rarely sold at stationery stores. After 1871, when postage rates dropped, the sending of Christmas cards became a general practice.

Christmas Cake

A fruited cake to celebrate the bounty of the harvest

Cake

1 cup sugar

1 cup butter or margarine

5 eggs, separated

1 cup raisins

1 cup golden raisins

1 cup dried currants

½ cup chopped almonds

½ cup chopped mixed candied fruit peel

½ cup candied cherries

4 teaspoons grated lemon peel

1 cup all-purpose flour

½ teaspoon baking powder

½ teaspoon ground allspice

1 teaspoon ground cinnamon

1 teaspoon ground ginger

Almond paste and icing

Jam or preserves (any flavor)

2 tubes (7 ounces each) almond paste

6 cups powdered sugar

3 pasteurized egg whites*

1 to 2 tablespoons lemon juice

1. Heat oven to 300°F. Grease a 9- or 10-inch springform pan; line bottom with wax paper. In large bowl, combine sugar and butter; beat until smooth and creamy. Add egg yolks; beat well. In small bowl, beat egg whites until stiff peaks form; fold into butter mixture. In medium bowl, mix raisins, golden raisins, currants, almonds, candied peel, candied cherries, and lemon peel. In another bowl, mix flour, baking powder, allspice, cinnamon, and ginger.

2. Alternately add flour mixture and fruit mixture to butter mixture, blending well after each addition. Spoon and spread mixture evenly in lined pan. Bake about 2 hours or until set and toothpick inserted in center comes out clean. Cool in pan 1 hour. Carefully remove cake from pan; place on wire rack to cool further. Refrigerate until very cold.

3. In small saucepan, heat jam until very warm. Brush top and sides of cake with jam. On powdered sugared surface, roll almond paste to ¼-inch thickness. Use base of springform pan to cut round of almond paste. Place almond paste round on cake. Cut strips to cover sides of cake with remaining almond paste. Pinch seams together to create a smooth covering. Let stand about 24 hours at room temperature or until set.

4. In medium bowl, combine powdered sugar and pasteurized egg whites; beat at high speed until well blended. Gradually add lemon juice, beating constantly until icing is thick, smooth, and very white. Spread icing over sides and top of cake. Let stand 2 to 3 hours or until set. If desired, decorate cake with cloth ribbon or add tiny figurines to form Christmas scene on top of cake.

Makes 1 cake, 12 to 16 servings.

Tip: Because the eggs are uncooked in this icing, regular egg whites are not recommended. Look for pasteurized egg whites where you buy eggs.

From *Christmas: The Annual of Christmas Literature and Art*, 1996, volume 66, page 63

DESSERTS

Serbian Blessings

An essential part of an old Serbian Christmas Day tradition was the coming of the *polaznik*, meaning "comer." The *polaznik* was a young boy from a neighboring village who arrived at a home at an early hour. As the door was opened to him, he cried out, *"Hristos se rodi,"* which means "Christ is born." He threw wheat over the room, over the people, and in all four corners. Then the mother of the household threw wheat back at him and everyone said, "In truth, he is born."

Next, the *polaznik* went to the hearth and stuck streams of sparks from the *Badnjak*, or Yule log, and said, "May you have this year as many cattle, horses, oxen, hogs, sheep, good luck, prosperity, and joy." The father embraced the boy. Then the boy laid down before the hearth, touched the unburned end of the *Badnjak* with his lips, and placed a coin upon it. Finally, the family offered presents to the *polaznik*, who was the guest of honor for the day.

Almond Torte

A meringue layer cake with chocolate frosting and almonds

Meringue

10 egg whites
1 cup sugar
1 cup ground almonds
$\frac{1}{4}$ cup unseasoned dry bread crumbs
2 teaspoons grated lemon peel
1 tablespoon lemon juice

Frosting

10 egg yolks
$\frac{3}{4}$ cup sugar
1 cup butter
3 ounces sweet or semisweet baking chocolate, chopped
2 tablespoons sliced almonds

1. Heat oven to 275ºF. Grease four 8- or 9-inch cake pans. Line bottom of pans with wax paper. In large bowl, beat egg whites with electric mixer at high speed until soft peaks form. (Set aside egg yolks.) Gradually add 1 cup of the sugar, beating until stiff glossy peaks form. Fold in ground almonds, bread crumbs, lemon peel, and lemon juice. Spread mixture evenly in the cake pans.

2. Bake meringues for 1 hour. Turn oven off; leave meringues in oven for 1 hour. (Meringues should be firm and dry to the touch.) Remove from oven; cool completely at room temperature.

3. Combine egg yolks and sugar and heat in double boiler over simmering water. Cook until thick and lemon colored, 10 to 15 minutes, beating constantly. Remove from heat. Beat in butter and chocolate until smooth. Cool slightly. Cover and refrigerate until chilled. (Mixture will thicken as it cools.)

4. Carefully remove meringues from pans. Spread chocolate mixture between layers; spread over top and sides. Sprinkle torte with sliced almonds.

Makes 1 cake, 12 to 16 servings.

From *Christmas: The Annual of Christmas Literature and Art*, 1957, volume 27, page 33

Christmas in America

The colonies' first immigrants brought their Christmas holiday traditions and love of feasting to America—that is, unless they were Puritans or Quakers. In 1621, Governor Bradford of the Plymouth Colony said that a Christmas celebration would not be tolerated. For Protestants, it was a relic from the time of the Reformation and therefore negatively associated with the Roman Catholic Church. As late as 1657 the General Court of Massachusetts assessed a penalty of five shillings for anyone who observed "any such day as Christmas or the like, either by forbearing of labor, feasting, or in any other way." Though this law was repealed in 1681, the feeling against the day persisted for a time.

In 1836, Alabama became the first state to declare Christmas a legal holiday; Louisiana and Arkansas followed. During the Civil War, New England's beloved poet Henry Wadsworth Longfellow wrote the now-familiar poem, which begins:

I heard the bells on Christmas Day
Their old, familiar carols play,
And wild and sweet
The words repeat
Of peace on earth, goodwill to men!

By 1890, December 25 was declared a legal holiday in all U.S. states and territories. In 1912, the first Christmas tree was erected in Madison Square in New York City.

Indian Pudding with Nutmeg Hard Sauce

A sweet Christmassy dessert

Pudding

6 cups milk
$\frac{1}{2}$ cup yellow cornmeal
1 egg
$\frac{3}{4}$ cup light molasses
$\frac{1}{4}$ cup butter, softened
3 tablespoons sugar
1 teaspoon salt
$\frac{1}{2}$ teaspoon ground mace
$\frac{1}{4}$ teaspoon ground ginger
$\frac{1}{4}$ teaspoon ground cloves
$\frac{1}{4}$ teaspoon ground nutmeg

Hard sauce

1 cup powdered sugar
$\frac{1}{3}$ cup butter, softened
1 teaspoon vanilla
$\frac{1}{2}$ teaspoon ground nutmeg

1. Heat oven to 250°F. In large saucepan, bring 4 cups of the milk just to a boil over medium-high heat. Reduce heat to medium-low. Add cornmeal gradually, stirring constantly. Cook 10 to 12 minutes or until mixture is thick, stirring frequently.

2. Beat egg in large bowl. Add molasses and $\frac{1}{4}$ cup butter; blend well. Add sugar, salt, mace, ginger, cloves, and $\frac{1}{4}$ teaspoon nutmeg; mix well. Stir in cornmeal mixture. Spoon and spread mixture in ungreased 2-quart casserole. Pour remaining 2 cups milk over the top. Do not stir.

3. Bake 4 to 5 hours or until set and crust forms over the top of the pudding.

4. Meanwhile, in medium bowl, beat all hard sauce ingredients until smooth. Cover and refrigerate until serving time. Serve warm pudding topped with spoonful of hard sauce.

Makes 8 servings.

From *Christmas: The Annual of Christmas Literature and Art*, 1972, volume 42, page 38

DESSERTS

History of Plum Pudding

Many Christmas customs from England originated in the Middle Ages when kings and noblemen ordered great feasts and celebrations. At these lavish medieval banquets, the boar's head was ceremoniously brought in and, as a crowning touch, a flaming plum pudding graced the table.

The legend of the first pudding is this: A king and his hunting party became lost in the forest on Christmas Eve. Since they had planned to be at their respective homes in time for the evening celebrations, they had taken only meager provisions with them. They decided to combine these provisions—small amounts of meat, ale, flour, brandy, sugar, and fruit—to make a dish that was shared by all members of the party. This concoction is said to have resulted in the first English Christmas pudding.

Plum Pudding

A molded, fragrant pudding

Pudding

3 ½ cups all-purpose flour
1 teaspoon baking soda
1 teaspoon salt
1 teaspoon ground cinnamon
½ teaspoon ground cloves
½ teaspoon ground nutmeg
1 cup buttermilk
1 cup molasses
1 cup raisins
1 cup dried currants
Hard sauce, see recipe page 55

Special equipment

2-quart pudding mold (or casserole dish that will fit
    inside a steamer)

1. Grease 2-quart pudding mold or casserole dish. In large bowl, mix flour, baking soda, salt, cinnamon, cloves, nutmeg, buttermilk, and molasses until well blended. Stir in raisins and currants. Spoon and spread mixture in pudding mold or dish. Cover with lid or foil.

2. Place mold on wire rack in large steamer or kettle. Add enough boiling water to steamer to come halfway up side of mold; cover steamer. Keep water boiling gently over low heat. If necessary, add water to maintain steam. Steam 2 ½ to 3 hours or until pudding springs back when touched lightly in center.

3. Meanwhile, prepare hard sauce as directed in recipe on page 55. Serve warm pudding topped with spoonful of hard sauce.

Makes 8 servings.

From *Christmas: The Annual of Christmas Literature and Art*, 1973, volume 43, page 39

A Danish Christmas Eve Dinner

Danes customarily would have celebrated with a big dinner after the Christmas Eve service. Greetings of *"Glædelig Jul!"* ("Merry Christmas!") resounded as members would leave church and go to their homes to enjoy festive dinners.

A number of traditional foods would await them. The Christmas goose—stuffed with prunes and apples—would be served with browned potatoes and fluffy rice. Almond pudding *(Ris Almande)* was often the dessert. This pudding would contain both chopped almonds and one whole almond. The person who would find the whole almond in their pudding was given a prize or would be honored by receiving the first gift. A bowl of the pudding was also put on the porch or in the barn for the *Nisser,* the Christmas elf. If the pudding was gone by morning, it was believed the household would have good luck during the coming year.

Later, family and friends would join hands and form a circle around the tree. The tree, often standing in the center of the room, would usually be trimmed with small paper Danish flags, cone-shaped cornucopias filled with small candies, tiny wreaths, garlands of bells made from colored paper or foil, and family ornaments.

Ris Almande

A sweet rice and almond pudding

Pudding

3 ½ cups milk
¾ cup long-grain white rice
¼ cup sugar
¼ cup sherry
2 teaspoons vanilla
1 cup blanched almonds, chopped
1 whole blanched almond
1 cup heavy whipping cream
Ground cinnamon, if desired

1. In medium saucepan, bring milk just to a boil. Stir in rice and sugar; mix well. Simmer uncovered over low heat for 20 to 30 minutes or until rice is tender, stirring occasionally.

2. Stir in sherry, vanilla, chopped almonds, and blanched almond. Cool. In medium bowl, beat cream until stiff peaks form. Fold whipped cream into rice mixture. Spoon into serving bowl. Refrigerate pudding until well chilled. Garnish with cinnamon if desired.

Makes 6 servings.

From *Christmas: The Annual of Christmas Literature and Art*, 1977, volume 47, page 48

Legend of the Thorn Tree

Christmas traditions are rich with symbolism, such as the number twelve, as in the twelve days of Christmas and the twelve apostles who spread the good news of Jesus. One symbol associated with the birth of Jesus is the thorn tree. Legend tells that Joseph of Arimathea—the man who provided a tomb for Jesus's body—came to England in 63 AD to convert the people of that land. There he placed his staff in the ground, and it grew into a thorn tree that bloomed every Christmas. A Puritan reformer is said to have destroyed the original tree, but a descendant of that tree still stands and blooms in Glastonbury, England. Such symbols do not replace the beautiful biblical story of the coming of Jesus into this world, but they do serve as a kind of shorthand, reminding us of humankind's expectation of a Savior and the fulfilling of those expectations on that first Christmas.

Twelve-Fruit Compote

A variety of sweet flavors in one dish

1 pound mixed dried fruits such as pears, figs, apricots, and
    peaches
1 cup pitted prunes
$\frac{1}{2}$ cup raisins or dried currants
3 cups water
1 cup pitted, canned sweet cherries with juice
2 medium apples, peeled and sliced
$\frac{1}{2}$ cup fresh or frozen cranberries
$\frac{1}{4}$ cup sugar
1 lemon, thinly sliced
6 whole cloves
2 cinnamon sticks
1 orange
$\frac{1}{2}$ cup seedless green or red grapes
$\frac{1}{2}$ cup fruit-flavored brandy or apple juice
$\frac{1}{2}$ cup pomegranate seeds

1. In 6- to 8-quart saucepan, combine dried fruit, prunes, raisins, and water. Bring to a boil. Reduce heat to low; cover and simmer 10 minutes, or until fruit is tender.

2. Add cherries with juice, apples, cranberries, sugar, lemon slices, cloves, and cinnamon. Cover and simmer 5 minutes, stirring occasionally. Remove from heat.

3. Grate peel from orange. Peel and section orange, removing skin and white membrane. Add grated peel and fruit to sauce. Stir in grapes and brandy. Cover and let stand about 15 minutes. Remove whole cloves, cinnamon sticks, and lemon pieces. Spoon fruit into serving bowl. Sprinkle with pomegranate seeds.

Makes 12 servings.

From *Christmas: The Annual of Christmas Literature and Art*, 1996, volume 66, page 63

Scottish *New Year's* Celebrations

In Scotland, New Year's Day is called *Hogmanay*, or Auld Year's Day. By tradition, whoever entered the door first after the clock rang in the New Year was called the "first footer." This person was believed to bring either good or bad luck to the household for the rest of the year. The best "first footer" was a handsome stranger. Sometimes a member of the family would go out and come back in as the "first footer," bringing traditional gifts that symbolize warmth and prosperity— bread, salt, a piece of coal, a few coins, and a sprig of evergreen.

One custom in parts of Scotland was to burn out the old year with great bonfires, around which people danced with lighted torches before partaking from the wassail bowl. It was thought best to begin New Year's Day the way you wanted the year itself to go: rising early, paying debts and borrowing no more, having plenty of money in your pocket, dining well, being cheerful, and determining to work hard. In the Scottish Highlands, generosity and good wishes often extended to extra portions for the animals.

Hogmanay Shortbread

Buttery, cut-out treats

Cookies

¾ cup unsalted butter or margarine
¼ cup sugar
2 cups all-purpose flour

Special equipment

Cookie cutters

1. Heat oven to 350°F. In medium bowl, combine butter and sugar; mix until light and fluffy. Add flour; mix with wooden spoon or hands until smooth and well combined.

2. On lightly floured surface, roll out dough to ¼- to ½-inch thickness. With cookie cutters, cut into desired shapes such as leaves, ovals, or squares. Flute edges of cookies as desired by pinching dough with fingers. Place on ungreased cookie sheet.

3. Bake 15 to 20 minutes or until set. (Tops of cookies will not be brown.)

Makes about 2 dozen cookies.

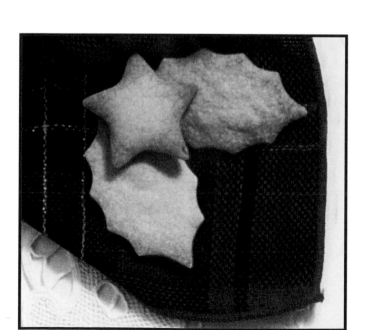

From *Christmas: The Annual of Christmas Literature and Art*, 1991, volume 61, page 28

Holiday of Light

Many of Sweden's old traditions involved light. By four o'clock on Christmas morning members of Swedish households would get up to light candles in every window to "light the Christ child on his way." Then it was off to church for *Jullotta*, a five o'clock morning worship service of light. In earlier days, people carried lighted torches to church that morning or attached them to their sleighs. The churches were lit with hundreds of candles. The remainder of Christmas Day was quiet, but on "Second Day Christmas," the social life of the community swelled to great proportions.

In Norwegian traditions, light was also significant during this season of darkness in Scandinavia. Men sometimes wore a star in their buttonholes, which star singers sold them on street corners. December 26, also a legal holiday, was often the occasion for the popular Christmas play for children, *Reisen til Julestjernen*, "The Search for the Christmas Star." The fairy tale tells of a king who, in his sorrow over his kidnapped daughter, banished the Christmas star.

Sandbakkels

Cup-shaped, buttery delights

Cookies

2 cups sugar
2 cups butter, softened
1 egg
1 teaspoon almond extract
4 ½ cups all-purpose flour

Special equipment

Sandbakkel molds or small tart tins

1. Heat oven to 375°F. In large bowl, beat sugar and butter until smooth. Add egg and almond extract; blend well. Stir in flour until well blended; knead with hands if necessary. Press small piece of dough into each sandbakkel mold to make very thin layer. (Cookies puff as they bake.) Place molds on cookie sheet.

2. Bake 10 to 15 minutes or until golden brown. Cool cookies in molds. To remove from molds, invert and tap bottom of mold gently with tableknife.

Makes about 8 dozen cookies with larger molds; 15 dozen with smaller molds.

From *Christmas: The Annual of Christmas Literature and Art*, 1963, volume 33, page 66

Greek Christmas Traditions

On Christmas Day, Greek tradition called for special visits to people with the name Chris, Christine, and Emmanuel, who would receive gifts. Open houses in their honor would have lasted the entire day. For the people of Greece, name days were cause for celebration, since Baptism is a reminder of spiritual birth.

Family gifts would be exchanged December 31 to usher in the New Year. January 1 is also the feast of Saint Basil, patron of Greece and an early father of the church who, when he became a Christian, gave up his wealth. Legend says he often baked bread with a coin inside for those in need. Therefore on New Year's Eve just before midnight, the family would share *Vasilópita* ("Basil's bread"). Whoever found a coin in his or her piece of bread would hope for special blessings in the new year.

Throughout the year, Greek children enjoy butter cookies called *kourabiethes*. At Christmastime, however, these cookies are coated in snowy powdered sugar and ornamented with a whole clove. The cloves, which are only decorative, symbolize the spices brought by the magi to the baby Jesus.

Kourabiethes

Snowy, powdered sugar–covered butter cookies

Cookies

1 cup butter, softened
½ cup granulated sugar
1 egg
½ teaspoon vanilla
½ teaspoon almond extract
2 ½ cups all-purpose flour
1 teaspoon baking powder
¼ teaspoon salt
Whole cloves, if desired (for decoration only)
Powdered sugar

1. Heat oven to 350ºF. In large bowl, combine butter, sugar, and egg; beat until light and fluffy. Beat in vanilla and almond extract. Add flour, baking powder, and salt; blend well.

2. For each cookie, shape ½ tablespoon of dough into ball, crescent, or S-shape. Place 2 inches apart on ungreased cookie sheet. Press whole clove in each cookie.

3. Bake 15 to 20 minutes or until edges are light golden brown. Remove cookies from cookie sheet; cool on wire racks. Sprinkle cooled cookies with powdered sugar. (Be sure guests remove any decorative cloves before eating cookies.)

Makes about 3 dozen cookies.

From *Christmas: The Annual of Christmas Literature and Art*, 1991, volume 61, page 26

Respect for the Animals

In Norway, the animals traditionally received special respect on Christmas Eve. At harvest time, farmers set aside the largest sheaves of grain; when Christmas arrived, they tied the sheaves to the top of a spruce pole, creating a Christmas tree for the birds. Norwegians believed the birds deserved a feast, too, since they were present at the Christ child's birth in the stable.

Fish and wild beasts, too, received regard during the holiday, as hunters removed all traps and snares and fishers hauled in their nets from the oceans and rivers. *Julenissen*, the legendary elf-like creature who was believed to live in the barn and help the household throughout the year, received a special bowl of *rømmegrøt* (a custard-like pudding) on Christmas Eve. Parents also rewarded children for their care of animals by serving up hot chocolate and *berlinerkranser* cookies.

Berlinerkranser

Puffy, wreath-shaped cookies

Cookies

4 hard-cooked egg yolks
4 uncooked egg yolks
1 cup sugar
2 cups unsalted butter
5 to 5 ½ cups all-purpose flour
1 egg white, beaten
Coarse decorator sugar

1. Mash hard-cooked egg yolks in large bowl. Add uncooked egg yolks and sugar; mix well. Add butter; blend until smooth. Add flour, 1 cup at a time, mixing well after each addition. If desired, cover and refrigerate 1 to 2 hours for easier handling.

2. Heat oven to 350ºF. On lightly floured surface, roll teaspoonfuls of dough into small ropes, about ½-inch in diameter. Form each rope into wreath shape, overlapping ends. Place about 1-inch apart on ungreased cookie sheets. Brush with beaten egg white; sprinkle with coarse sugar.

3. Bake 10 to 14 minutes or until edges are light golden brown. Remove from cookie sheets. Cool cookies on wire racks.

Makes about 8 dozen cookies.

From *Christmas: The Annual of Christmas Literature and Art*, 1963, volume 33, page 64

Homemade Trees and Cookies

Because Iceland has few trees, years ago, Icelandic people would make their own Christmas trees. They used a pole as the center trunk and fastened shorter poles onto it as branches. If the snow thawed, families hauled in armloads of shrub branches with foliage, such as cedar, and fastened these to the framework. Decorated with homemade colored-paper ornaments and old-fashioned candles, the homemade tree assumed a genuinely festive air.

One traditional Icelandic cookie favorite is *half-manar* (half-moon) cookies, which are flavored with a spice commonly used for Christmas baking in Iceland—cardamom. The Vikings first brought cardamom to Iceland centuries ago; they discovered this unique flavoring on their sailing expeditions through Middle Eastern spice-trading centers.

Halfmanar

A fluffy, filled cookie shaped like a half-moon

Cookies

2 ½ cups all-purpose flour
⅔ cup sugar
1 teaspoon ground cardamom
½ teaspoon baking powder
½ teaspoon hartshorn (ammonium bicarbonate)*
1 ⅓ cups butter or margarine
1 egg, beaten
1 can (10 ounces) plum (or prune) butter (also called lekvar)

1. In large bowl, combine flour, sugar, cardamom, baking powder, and hartshorn. Cut butter into small pieces; add to flour mixture. Mix with pastry blender or two forks until well combined. Add egg; mix well. Cover dough and refrigerate 1 hour for easier handling.

2. Heat oven to 350ºF. Grease cookie sheets. On well-floured surface, roll dough to ⅛- ¼-inch thickness. Cut rounds with cookie cutter or rim of glass dipped in flour. Place on greased cookie sheets. Place about ½ teaspoon plum butter on each dough round. Fold dough over filling to make half-moon shapes. Press round edge of each cookie with fork dipped in flour to seal.

3. Bake 10 to 15 minutes or until edges start to brown. Remove from cookie sheets; cool on wire racks.

Makes 5 to 6 dozen cookies, depending on size.

Tip: Hartshorn, a white powder available at most drugstores, is used as a leavening agent in these cookies. The predecessor of baking powder and baking soda, hartshorn is still called for in some cookie recipes as it provides a "fluffiness" that the other agents do not. If your drugstore carries this in granular form, be sure to grind it to a fine powder before using. It may give off an ammonia odor while the dough is raw or baking, but this will not be smelled or tasted in the cookies themselves. If you are unable to find hartshorn, you may substitute an equal amount of baking powder.

From *Christmas: The Annual of Christmas Literature and Art*, 1991, volume 61, page 31

The Jultomter

In Swedish Christmas lore, the *jultomter* are said to be tiny gnome-like figures whose permanent lodging on farms and in villages is in barns, though sometimes you can hear them creeping over attic floors and up and down stairs. All through the year they keep busy tending sick cattle. When danger is afoot, they notify the farmer with a nudge. They are the last to retire at night, making sure that all doors are locked and that lamps and candles are out. Families in Sweden would not think of sitting down to a bountiful Christmas Eve supper before they set out a bowl of hot milk for the jultomter. Then at midnight this red-clad figure with pointed cap and long white beard rides into the house astride a goat, carrying gifts for everyone.

Krumkake

A thin cookie baked in an iron then rolled to form a tube

Cookies

3 eggs
³/₄ cup sugar
1 teaspoon vanilla
1 teaspoon ground cardamom (optional)
½ cup butter, melted
1 cup plus 2 tablespoons all-purpose flour

Special equipment

Krumkake iron
Krumkake form or thick wooden handle

1. Heat krumkake iron over medium-low to medium burner. In large bowl, beat eggs with electric mixer on medium speed until thick and lemon-colored, about 5 minutes. Gradually add sugar, beating well after each addition. Beat in vanilla and cardamom. Alternately add butter and flour, beating constantly.

2. For each krumkake, drop about 1 teaspoon batter on hot krumkake iron; lower top of iron and flip iron. (Turning iron keeps heat even on both sides.) Bake until light golden brown. Carefully remove krumkake from iron with tableknife; immediately roll on wooden form or end of wooden spoon to make a tube. Cool cookies on wire racks.

Makes about 4 to 4 ½ dozen cookies.

From *Christmas: The Annual of Christmas Literature and Art*, 1963, volume 33, page 64

Old English Traditions

Roman, medieval, and Gothic ages of the British Isles have given rise to numerous quaint Christmas festivities. Christianity took hold in England in the sixth to eighth centuries. The English tradition of mumming at Christmastide is more than one thousand years old. Dressed in costume and wearing paper masks, mummers enact ancient rituals; mimic such historic figures as Oliver Cromwell, Lord Nelson, or Napoleon; or perhaps characterize Saint George doing battle with Beelzebub. In Hampshire, mummers, sometimes with grotesque faces of papier-mâché or wood, enact whole plays.

Today's custom of a Christmas tree replaced an old English custom, the kissing bough. The kissing bough was a double hoop covered with greenery, candles, apples, small gifts, and ornaments; the hoops were hung from the ceiling in a notable spot in every cottage. From the bottom of the kissing bough hung a sprig of mistletoe. Many kissing boughs included figures of Mary, Joseph, and the Christ child, thereby serving as England's version of the crèche.

Brandy Snaps

Cone-shaped shells filled with flavored whipped cream

Cookies

¾ cup unsalted butter
⅔ cup light corn syrup
¼ cup firmly packed brown sugar
1 ¼ teaspoons ground ginger
Dash salt
1 cup all-purpose flour
4 teaspoons brandy (or 1 teaspoon brandy extract plus
   3 teaspoons water)

Filling

2 cups heavy whipping cream
1 tablespoon sugar
2 teaspoons brandy, if desired
1 teaspoon vanilla

Special equipment

Krumkake form, cannoli mold, or thick wooden handle
Pastry tube and tips (or plastic bags) to pipe icing

1. Heat oven to 350ºF. Grease cookie sheets. In heavy saucepan, combine butter, corn syrup, brown sugar, ginger, and salt. Bring to a boil, stirring frequently. Remove from heat. Stir in flour and 4 teaspoons brandy (or substitute). To keep batter warm, place saucepan in pan of hot water.

2. Drop batter by tablespoonfuls onto greased cookie sheets. (Batter will spread, so bake only 4 cookies at a time.) Bake 7 to 10 minutes or until deep golden brown. Cool 1 minute; remove from cookie sheets. Immediately roll each cookie around wooden form or end of wooden spoon; press seam with fingers to seal. (Krumkake form or cannoli mold can be used.) Cool cookies on wire rack. (If cookies become too stiff to bend, reheat briefly in oven.)

3. In large bowl, combine all filling ingredients; beat until stiff peaks form. Spoon whipped cream into pastry bag. Pipe whipped cream into cookies. Store in refrigerator for up to 2 hours before serving.

Makes 2 dozen cookies.

From *Christmas: The Annual of Christmas Literature and Art*, 1992, volume 62, page 52

Celebrating the Virgin Mary

The Virgin Mary is a central figure of the Christmas story, though she most likely was the daughter of a poor man in the village of Nazareth. Mary's song in Luke 1 tells of her lowly estate and of God's greatness. Indications are that she may have been no more than a mere servant, tending cattle and the house.

The Feast of the Immaculate Conception, honoring the Virgin Mary, eclipses the Christmas festival in some parts of Italy. Held December 8, the festival celebrates the occasion when the angel Gabriel visited Mary. Gabriel was the chief angel of the heavenly host, who had carried a message to Zechariah telling him that his wife Elizabeth would give birth to a son, John the Baptist. As recorded in Luke's Gospel, he was also sent to make the amazing announcement to Mary, that she would give birth to God's Son, Jesus.

Noché

Crisp-fried, honey- and sugar-coated bows

Cookies

5 eggs
2 cups all-purpose flour
2 tablespoons sugar
Oil for deep-frying
Honey, if desired
Coarse decorator sugar, if desired

Special equipment

Pinwheel cutter (or sharp knife)

1. In large bowl, beat eggs with electric mixer on medium speed until thick and lemon-colored; about 5 minutes or longer. Add flour and sugar; mix well. Place dough on lightly floured surface. Knead dough 3 to 5 minutes or until smooth.

2. Roll dough to ⅛-inch thickness. With pinwheel cutter or sharp knife, cut strips 2- to 2 ½-inches long and 1-inch wide. Pinch each strip in center to resemble bow.

3. Heat 2 to 3 inches oil in large deep skillet or deep fryer to 350ºF. Drop noché into oil, a few at a time. Cook until golden brown, turning once if necessary. Drain on paper towels. If desired, just before serving drizzle cooled cookies with honey and sprinkle with coarse sugar.

Makes about 3 dozen cookies.

From *Christmas: The Annual of Christmas Literature and Art*, 1978, volume 48, page 18

St. Francis and the Crèche

On a hillside outside of Greccio, Italy, in the 13th century, Francis of Assisi created the first manger scene. Francis withdrawn for a time from the duties and responsibilities of the rapidly growing order of Poor Friars. In his s mountaintop retreat, he spent time in prayer. As Christmas approached, he wanted to relive the birth of Christ so he himself might become more Christlike. He also wanted to bring alive the humility of Christ's birth for others. believed that understanding how God became poor for humanity's sake would cause hearts to be filled with grati and people to gladly share with the poor and the hungry, even giving their animals an extra portion of hay.

He converted a cave on a hillside into a manger, which included a live ox and donkey. Costumed villagers represe Mary and Joseph and the other members of the nativity story. On Christmas Eve, people gathered before the st sang hymns, and celebrated a simple mass. The first manger scene so moved all who saw it that the custom rap spread. By tradition the crèche (also called the *praesepio*) would be the focal point of an Italian Christmas.

Calgionetti

A fried, chocolate-and-nut-filled cookie

Filling

1 pound fresh chestnuts, shells removed
1 cup chopped walnuts
4 ounces sweet baking chocolate, finely chopped (about 1 cup)
1 cup corn syrup

Crust

6 cups all-purpose flour
2 teaspoons baking powder
½ teaspoon salt
1 cup white or rose wine
1 cup vegetable oil
2 eggs
Oil for deep-frying
Powdered sugar

Special equipment

Pinwheel cutter (or sharp knife)

1. In large saucepan combine shelled chestnuts and enough water to cover. Bring to a boil. Reduce heat to medium; cook 10 to 15 minutes or until soft. In large bowl, mash chestnuts. Stir in walnuts, chocolate, and corn syrup. (Mixture will have a pasty consistency.)

2. In another large bowl, combine flour, baking powder, and salt. Add wine, 1 cup oil, and eggs; mix until well combined. Place dough on lightly floured surface. Knead dough 3 to 5 minutes or until smooth.

3. Roll dough to ⅛-inch thickness. Starting with edge of dough nearest you, drop heaping teaspoons of filling about 1 inch apart in row. Fold dough over row of filling. Cut with pinwheel cutter or sharp knife around filled portion. Crimp edges with fork. Continue to drop filling in rows, folding dough, cutting, and crimping to edge of dough. Reroll dough as necessary.

4. Heat 2 to 3 inches oil in large deep skillet or deep fryer to 350°F. Drop calgionetti into oil, a few at a time. Cook until golden brown, turning if necessary. Drain on paper towels. Cool completely. Sprinkle cooled cookies with powdered sugar.

Makes about 4 dozen cookies.

From *Christmas: The Annual of Christmas Literature and Art*, 1978, volume 48, page 18

Dining Traditions

Only a minority of the population practice Christianity in China, but holidays are usually observed with great ceremony. Guests at dinner, seated eight to a table, traditionally would seek out the humblest seat. The place of honor would be the right-hand seat at the head of the table. The humblest seat would be the chair closest to the door, where the host would sit to receive the bowls of food and place them on the table. According to etiquette, everyone would act as if he or she wanted to sit closest to the door. The host would usually solve the difficulty by insisting that it was his chair. The guest of honor would generally be determined by one of two things. That person would either be the one who came the greatest distance or the one who had the greatest seniority. When the seat of honor had been taken, the other guests would place themselves accordingly.

Once the guests were seated, the host would pick up his chopsticks; this would be the signal for others to do the same. The first course would usually consist of eight varieties of cold dishes and the second course eight varieties of hot foods. The last course at a fancy feast would be rice and cabbage. Until Westerners introduced sweets, Chinese people traditionally did not eat them.

Hang Geen Beng*

A sliced almond cookie

Cookies
½ cup lard, shortening, or butter**
¼ cup plus 2 tablespoons sugar
½ teaspoon almond or vanilla extract
1 cup all-purpose flour
½ teaspoon salt

Topping
1 egg yolk
1 tablespoon water
¼ cup blanched almonds

1. In large bowl, combine lard, sugar, and extract; beat until smooth. Add flour and salt; mix well. (Use hands, if necessary, to blend well.) Shape dough into long log, 1-inch in diameter. Wrap in wax paper. Refrigerate 1 hour.

2. Heat oven to 400°F. Lightly grease cookie sheets. Cut dough into ¼-inch slices. Place 1-inch apart on greased cookie sheets. In small bowl, beat egg yolk and water. Brush over top of cookies. Press an almond half in top of each cookie.

3. Bake 8 to 10 minutes or until light golden brown. Cool 1 to 2 minutes on pan; remove from cookie sheet. Cool on wire racks.

Makes about 2 dozen cookies.

Tip: This is pronounced hahng geen bee-EHNG.
**Tip: As dairy products were rare in China, these cookies were traditionally made with lard. They can be made with butter or margarine, but the flavor will be somewhat different.*

From *Christmas: The Annual of Christmas Literature and Art*, 1991, volume 61, page 29

Angel-like Gift Bearers

According to custom, *Christkind*, the Christ child's messenger, would deliver gifts to children in the German state of Bavaria. He or she would wander through the Christmas Eve snow with presents for everyone. The *Christkind* would often be represented by a child dressed in white robes with big golden wings and wearing a golden crown. Families would place candles in their windows to light the *Christkind's* way. Similarly, an angel-like *Christkindli* would visit the children of Switzerland to bring them gifts of fruit and nuts.

Among the inhabitants of these mountain regions, the week between Christmas and New Year's Day was traditionally set aside for visiting family and friends. It would be common for two or even three generations to gather in a single house to exchange gifts and share in food and friendship.

Zimsterne

Thin and crispy cinnamon stars

Cookies

1 ½ cups sugar
3 tablespoons butter or margarine, softened
1 teaspoon lemon juice
2 whole eggs
1 egg, separated
2 ⅓ cups all-purpose flour
2 ½ teaspoons baking powder
¼ teaspoon salt
1 ¼ teaspoons ground cinnamon
¼ teaspoon ground nutmeg
½ cup finely chopped walnuts

Special equipment

3-inch star cookie cutter

1. Heat oven to 375°F. Lightly grease cookie sheets. In large bowl, combine sugar, butter, lemon juice, whole eggs, and 1 egg yolk; beat until light and fluffy. Add all remaining ingredients except walnuts; mix well. Stir in walnuts. Cover dough with plastic wrap. Chill for 15 minutes.

2. On lightly floured surface, roll out ⅓ of dough at a time to ¹⁄₁₆-inch thickness. Cut dough with 3-inch star cookie cutter. Place cut-outs on greased cookie sheets. In small bowl, beat egg white until frothy. Brush over tops of cookies.

3. Bake 6 to 8 minutes or until light golden brown. Remove from cookie sheets; cool on wire racks.

Makes 6 dozen cookies.

From *Christmas: The Annual of Christmas Literature and Art*, 1991, volume 61, page 27

Brazilian Traditions

At Christmas, making the *pesebre*, or manger scene, was a tradition in Brazil. Brightly colored sand would be used to form hills and plains for the manger scene. On Christmas Eve the Christ child would be placed in the crib and, beginning on Christmas Day, the magi would be moved forward a little each day to symbolize their journey from the East to Bethlehem.

On Christmas Eve, the family would gather to sing carols and hymns. As the tree was trimmed, parents would tell the Christmas story in words simple enough for even the youngest child to understand. Before going to bed, the children would place their shoes under the tree for Papa Noel to fill with toys and treats.

Misa de Gallo, Midnight Mass, was typical for many Brazilian Christians on Christmas Eve. Worshipers would bring gifts of food, wrapped in white paper, for people in need and lay them in a simple manger at the front of the church.

Lace Wafers

A nutty cookie with a candy-like texture

Cookies

1 ½ cups firmly packed light brown sugar
¼ cup butter, softened
2 tablespoons water
1 cup all-purpose flour
1 teaspoon ground cinnamon
1 ½ cups finely chopped Brazil nuts

1. Heat oven to 325°F. Grease cookie sheets. In large bowl, combine brown sugar and butter; beat until well mixed. Beat in water. Add flour and cinnamon; mix well. Stir in nuts.

2. Shape mixture into 40 to 60 (½- to 1-inch) balls; place 2 inches apart on greased cookie sheets.

3. Bake 15 to 20 minutes or until cookies flatten and are browned on the edges. Cool several minutes; remove from cookie sheet. Cool on wire racks. Store in airtight container.

Makes 4 to 5 dozen cookies.

From *Christmas: The Annual of Christmas Literature and Art,* 1991, volume 61, page 28

Cradle-rocking

In the 14th century, people in southern Germany started a Christmas custom in connection with the Christmas crib, or crèche. This was the practice of *Kindel* or cradle-rocking. In the church, members set up a cradle containing a representation of the Christ child. During the Christmas service, the clergy and choir took turns rocking the cradle and singing lullabies to the baby, while other people danced around the cradle. Later, members of the congregation also came to take turns rocking the baby. They would join in singing Christmas carols.

Martin Luther, the 16th-century church reformer, composed his affectionate Christmas hymn, "Vom Himmel hoch da komm ich her," or "From Heaven Above to Earth I Come," for this purpose. Sixteen stanzas, set to a well-known folk tune, tell the story of the infant Jesus.

From Heaven above to earth I come
To bear good news to every home
Glad tidings of great joy I bring
Whereof I now will say and sing

Hazelnut Cookies

A nutty, frosted cookie

Cookies
3 cups hazelnuts (about 1 ½ pounds), divided
8 egg whites
2 ¼ cups sugar
½ teaspoon vanilla

Glaze
1 cup powdered sugar
1 to 2 tablespoons water

1. Place 2 cups of the hazelnuts in food processor bowl; process until ground. Set aside remaining whole hazelnuts.

2. In large bowl, beat egg whites with electric mixer until stiff. Continue beating for 30 minutes, gradually adding sugar while beating. Stir in vanilla and ground hazelnuts until well blended. Cover and refrigerate 2 to 3 hours or overnight for easier handling.

3. Heat oven to 300ºF. Line cookie sheets with parchment paper. Drop hazelnut mixture by teaspoonfuls onto paper 1 inch apart. Press whole hazelnut into center of each cookie. Bake 1 hour or until cookies can be easily lifted from paper. Place on wire racks.

4. In medium bowl, mix powdered sugar and enough water for desired drizzling consistency. Drizzle warm cookies with glaze. Let stand until set.

Makes about 7 dozen cookies.

From *Christmas: The Annual of Christmas Literature and Art*, 1963, volume 33, page 62

A Cow's-Eye View of Christmas

by Dawn Finlay

I was a cow in the year number one,
and the first Christmas Day had only begun;
the rooster crowed and up came the sun.
I went to the door, as I did every day,
to stand in line for my breakfast hay
and listen to what the donkey might say.

The donkey was there and a pigeon or two,
so I greeted them all with a bright morning "Moo."
The donkey brayed, and the pigeons said, "Coo!"
We waited and waited for ever-so-long,
and the sweet smell of hay was ever-so-strong,
and someone was singing a lullaby song!

The stable looked different (but there was no danger)—
a beautiful lady sat by the manger.
Well, that was strange, but something was stranger!
The sweetest tiny baby lay
sound asleep in my breakfast hay.
That's when I bowed my head to pray.

Then as I knelt on the floor's hard sod,
I somehow knew—though this was odd—
I knew that the babe was the Son of God!
"God," I prayed (but it came out "Moo"),
"O God, what wonderful things you do!"
The donkey brayed, but the pigeons said, "Coo!"

From *Christmas: The Annual of Christmas Literature and Art*,
1991, volume 61, page 22-23

*Kanya**

No-bake peanut bars

Cookies

½ cup superfine sugar
½ cup creamy peanut butter
⅔ cup uncooked cream of rice cereal

1. Line 8 x 4-inch pan with plastic wrap or wax paper. In medium bowl, combine sugar and peanut butter; mix until smooth and well blended. Gradually add cereal; beating well after each addition.

2. Spoon and spread mixture in pan; press evenly. Cover with plastic wrap or wax paper. Refrigerate 2 to 3 hours or until firm. Carefully remove from pan. Cut into small bars.

Makes 1 pan, about 20 bars.

* *Tip: This is pronounced KAHN-yah.*

From *Christmas: The Annual of Christmas Literature and Art*, 1991, volume 61, page 29

The Wilia Meal

On Christmas Eve in Poland the *wilia* supper was traditionally rich in symbolism. *Wilia* means "to watch." No one would eat a meal during the day; the fast would be broken either when the first star appeared or at midnight. At that moment, folklore claimed, the earth itself responded: water in wells would turn to wine, animals would acquire human tongues, and blades of grass would greet each other. This would be the hour of peace on earth, goodwill among all people.

The *wilia* supper would traditionally be a twelve-course meal, meatless but with a large variety of fish to satisfy the appetites of the household. When the youngest child spotted the first star, the family would break the *oplatek*, a specially prepared unleavened bread. *Oplatek* dates back to the 10th century in Poland, the making of which evolved into an art form. The wafer-thin creations were made in iron plates forged with interlacing designs of wings, crosses, and stars. Some people would hang these ornaments from thread over the *wilia* Christmas table; others would dangle them from boughs of a Christmas tree. When the *oplatek* was broken, pieces would be exchanged and eaten as a family communion.

Mazurkas

A jam-covered pan cookie

Cookie

2 cups blanched almonds
1 cup unsalted butter or margarine
1 cup granulated sugar
4 eggs
2 tablespoons milk
2 cups all-purpose flour
¼ teaspoon salt

Topping

1 cup any flavor jam or preserves (such as apricot, raspberry, or
    strawberry)
Powdered sugar

1. Heat oven to 350ºF. Grease 15 x 10 x 1-inch baking pan. Place almonds in food processor bowl; process until ground. Set aside.

2. In large bowl, combine butter and granulated sugar; beat until smooth and creamy. Add eggs, one at a time, beating well after each addition. Beat in milk. Add flour gradually, beating slowly until well blended. Stir in salt and ground almonds. Spread mixture evenly over bottom of greased pan.

3. Bake 20 to 30 minutes or until golden brown. Remove from oven. Spoon and spread jam over warm crust. Cool about 5 minutes. Cut into bars. Cool completely on wire rack. Just before serving, sprinkle bars with powdered sugar.

Makes 70 2- by 1-inch bars.

From *Christmas: The Annual of Christmas Literature and Art*, 1991, volume 61, page 27

Town Celebrations

Communities in Northern Germany traditionally observed the Feast of Saint Lucia on December 13. Yet instead of following the Swedish practice of having a daughter serve family members coffee and cakes in bed, German celebrations were community events. School children would join together that evening for a *lichterzug*, a lantern procession through downtown. Created by the children in their crafts classes, the lanterns were often made out of wooden or wire skeletons covered with stretched material, painted colorfully. Sometimes the lanterns took the form of dollhouses; the candlelight would spill out windows as the children walked through the streets.

Another old German observance was the festival of light, when the whole community gathered on a hilltop on December 21, the winter solstice. According to former practice, a huge wheel was stuffed with straw, then torched and rolled down the hill like a dying sun, spinning bits of flame in all directions until coming to rest and to extinction in the dark valley below.

Pfeffernüesse

"Pepper nut" cookies

Cookies

2 ¼ cups firmly packed brown sugar
4 eggs
4 cups all-purpose flour
3 teaspoons baking powder
2 teaspoons ground cinnamon
2 teaspoons ground cloves
1 teaspoon ground nutmeg
½ teaspoon black pepper
1 ½ cups chopped walnuts
1 ½ cups dried currants

1. Heat oven to 350ºF. Grease cookie sheets. In large bowl, combine brown sugar and eggs; beat well. Add flour, baking powder, cinnamon, cloves, nutmeg, and pepper; mix well. Stir in walnuts and currants.

2. Shape dough into 1-inch balls; place on cookie sheets 1 inch apart. Bake 12 to 18 minutes or until golden brown. Immediately remove from cookie sheets. Cool cookies on wire racks.

Makes about 6 dozen cookies.

From *Christmas: The Annual of Christmas Literature and Art*, 1967, volume 37, page 52

Scandinavian Decorations

Scandinavians traditionally used straw for many of their Christmas decorations. The *julbuks*, a goat made from straw, was one of the most common. A Norwegian family also may have woven a straw crown and suspended it from the ceiling above their Christmas tree.

The tree itself was the real symbol of Christmas in Scandinavia. At one time, families would place three candles at the top of the tree to represent the magi; in the lower branches, they would hang decorations of people and animals important to the harvest. Through the year, Swedish families would save pretty bits of gold, silver, and colored paper to wrap homemade caramels, an essential for a Swedish Christmas. Dozens of tiny, gaily wrapped parcels would be prominent among the trimmings.

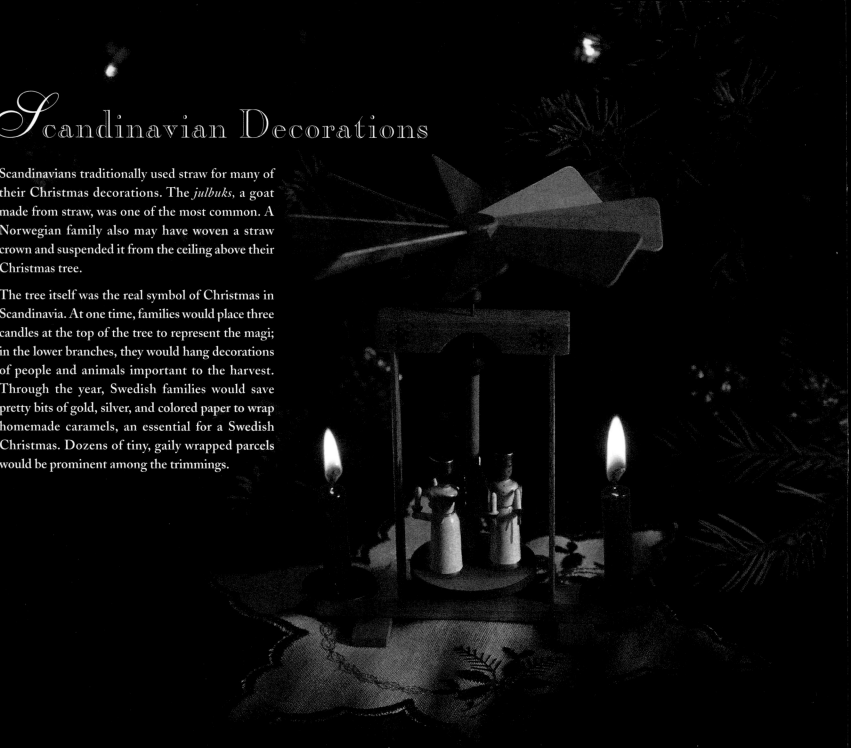

Kransekake

A frosted cookie tower

Cake

18 ounces blanched or unblanched almonds
4 cups powdered sugar
3 large egg whites

Glaze

3 cups powdered sugar
3 tablespoons butter, softened
1 teaspoon vanilla
4 to 6 tablespoons milk

Special equipment

Kransekake ring molds*

1. Heat oven to 325ºF. Butter and flour 16 kransekake ring molds. Place almonds in food processor bowl; process until ground. In large bowl, mix ground almonds, 4 cups powdered sugar and the egg whites until well blended (using dough hook on electric mixer, if possible). Cover with plastic wrap. Chill at least 1 hour.

2. Cut portions of dough and knead with hands until smooth. (Cover remaining dough to keep from drying out.) Roll dough with fingers into ropes the width of your little finger. Fit dough into molds, smoothing dough where ends meet. (Dough will puff out while baking.) Place molds on cookie sheet. (You will not be able to bake all the molds at once.)

3. Bake 10 to 15 minutes or until light golden brown. Cool cakes in molds.

4. In large bowl, mix 3 cups powdered sugar, butter, vanilla, and enough milk for desired drizzling consistency. If desired, place glaze in resealable plastic bag; cut small hole from corner to drizzle.

5. To assemble kransekake, layer cake rings on serving platter with largest ring at the bottom. Drizzle glaze in zigzag design over each ring before adding the next one. Let stand until set.

Makes 1 kransekake.

Tip: If you don't have the kransekake ring molds, cover cookie sheets with parchment paper. Cut off portions of the dough and shape into 16 to 18 ropes about the thickness of your little finger and a variety of lengths, from 4 to 22 inches. Shape each into a circle and place on the parchment paper. Bake and cool as directed above.

From *Christmas: The Annual of Christmas Literature and Art*, 1963, volume 33, page 66

The Cookie War

Baking cookies in the shapes of animal, dwarves, and stars was a centuries-old practice throughout the region of Germany, Holland, and Bavaria. *Lebkuchen*, considered a specialty of this area, were made as early as the beginning of the 15th century. An unwritten law said that this flavorful cookie should be only eaten at Christmastime; in some areas, the cookies could not be bought after New Year's Day.

So distinctive was this delight that some bakers specialized in making *Lebkuchen*. Rivalry was high. In Nuremberg in 1808, a fight broke out between the bread-and-cake makers and the *Lebkuchen* bakers. This uprising led to the so-called *Lebkuchen-Krieg* (war), which the king himself had to mediate. He made it a law that *Lebkuchen* should only be baked by *Lebkuchen* bakers and no one else.

Lebkuchen

A chewy, spicy cookie topped with an almond

Cookies

2 ¼ cups firmly packed brown sugar
1 ½ cups shortening
½ cup strong brewed coffee
2 tablespoons fresh lemon juice
2 eggs
7 cups all-purpose flour
1 teaspoon baking powder
½ teaspoon baking soda
½ teaspoon salt
1 teaspoon ground cinnamon
½ teaspoon ground cloves
½ teaspoon ground allspice
½ cup finely chopped blanched almonds
½ cup finely chopped candied citron*
1 tablespoon grated lemon peel
¼ to ½ cup sliced almonds

Special equipment

Heart-shaped cookie cutter, or as desired

1. In large bowl, combine brown sugar and shortening. Beat until creamy. Add coffee, lemon juice, and eggs; blend well. In second bowl, mix all dry ingredients except sliced almonds. Slowly mix into wet ingredients until well blended. (Dough should be quite stiff.) Cover and refrigerate dough for at least 8 hours.

2. Heat oven to 350°F. On floured surface, roll dough to ⅛- to ¼-inch thickness. Cut with floured 2-inch heart-shaped cookie cutter. Place on cookie sheet. Top each cookie with sliced almond.

3. Bake 7 to 10 minutes or until set. Cool 1 minute; remove from cookie sheets. Cool cookies on wire racks.

Makes about 9 to 10 dozen cookies.

* Tip: If unable to find candied citron, candied ginger is a good substitution in this recipe.

From *Christmas: The Annual of Christmas Literature and Art*, 1963, volume 33, page 63

Baking Day

For many people, one of the first harbingers of the coming holy season is the great baking day. Traditionally, Scandinavian homes became virtual bakeries from the middle of December and on. People believed one must have a plentiful supply of treats, for during the Christmas season, every visitor to one's home must be fed lest he or she "bear the Yule spirit from the house." That would be tragedy, for you cannot recapture the Yule spirit until the next year.

A popular cut-out cookie—gingersnaps—are known as *Pepparkakor* in Sweden, *Brunekager* in Denmark, *Piparkakut* in Finland, and *Pepperkaker* in Norway. Traditionally a variety of cookie cutters are used; each shape has meaning. Bell-shaped cookies represent the proclamation of good news, "Christ is born!" Star-shaped cookies either represent Jesus as "the bright morning star" (Revelation 22:16) or they represent the star that led the magi to the infant Jesus.

Pepparkakor

A spicy, cut-out gingersnap

Cookies

1 ½ cups sugar
⅔ cup sour cream
½ cup butter, softened
¾ cup dark corn syrup
3 ½ cups all-purpose flour
1 tablespoon baking powder
2 teaspoons ground cinnamon
1 teaspoon ground cloves
1 ½ teaspoons ground ginger

Special equipment

Cookie cutters

1. In large bowl, combine sugar, sour cream, butter, and corn syrup; beat until well blended. Add flour, baking powder, cinnamon, cloves, and ginger; mix well. Cover and refrigerate 8 hours or overnight.

2. Heat oven to 400°F. Grease cookie sheets. On well-floured surface, roll dough to ¼-inch thickness. Cut dough with desired cookie cutters. Place on greased cookie sheets.

3. Bake 8 to 10 minutes or until set. Cool 1 minute; remove from cookie sheets. Cool on wire racks.

Makes about 7 dozen cookies, depending on size of cookie cutter.

From *Christmas: The Annual of Christmas Literature and Art*, 1991, volume 61, page 30

CHRISTMAS

by Cleoral Lovell

C is for the Christ child sleeping on the hay;
H is for the heavenly host who came to earth that day.
R is for the radiance on Mary's holy face;
I is for the lowly inn, a poor and humble place.
S is for the star that shone to guide the shepherds there;
T is for the travelers bringing treasures rare.
M is for the manger, where he laid his little head;
A is for the angels guarding 'round his bed.
S is for the Savior who once lived on this earth;
Oh, wondrous day we celebrate, the day of Jesus's birth!

From *Christmas: The Annual of Christmas Literature and Art*, 1993, volume 63, page 64

Gingerbread Gift Box and Cookies

A twist on traditional gingerbread houses

Gingerbread

1 cup firmly packed brown sugar
1 cup butter, softened
1 cup light molasses
2 eggs
5 cups all-purpose flour
2 teaspoons baking soda
2 teaspoons ground cinnamon
1 ½ teaspoons ground allspice
1 teaspoon ground nutmeg
1 teaspoon ground cloves

Icing

4 cups powdered sugar
½ teaspoon cream of tartar
3 pasteurized egg whites*
1 teaspoon vanilla

Special equipment

Cardboard to make box pattern
Cookie cutters, such as traditional gingerbread "people"
Pastry tube and tips (or plastic bags) to pipe icing
Ribbon
Decorations

1. In large bowl, combine brown sugar and butter; beat until light and fluffy. Add molasses and eggs; blend well. In second bowl, mix dry ingredients. Slowly mix dry ingredients into wet ingredients; blend well. Cover and refrigerate at least 3 hours or until firm.

2. To make patterns for gift box, cut a 7 x 7-inch square and a 6 x 4-inch rectangle from cardboard. Dust pieces with flour to prevent them from sticking to dough.

3. Heat oven to 350ºF. Grease cookie sheets. On lightly floured surface, roll dough to ¼-inch thickness. Use cardboard patterns to cut out two squares for top and bottom of box and four rectangles for sides. Chill and reroll dough as necessary. Cut remaining dough with desired cookie cutters (such as traditional gingerbread "people") to make cookies to place in finished box. Place cutouts on greased cookie sheets.

4. Bake sides and bottom of box 15 to 17 minutes or until edges just begin to brown. Bake other cookies 8 to 12 minutes. Carefully remove from cookie sheets; cool on wire racks.

5. In large bowl, mix icing ingredients. Beat at high speed with electric mixer 9 to 10 minutes or until firm. While building box, cover icing bowl with wet towel.

6. To assemble gift box, vertically wrap each side rectangle in center with ribbon; tie on back side or secure with dab of icing. Wrap top square with ribbon in crisscross design, securing on underside of top piece. With round pastry tube tip, decorate sides and top pieces of box with icing as desired. Let stand until set.

7. Place bottom square on serving platter. (If desired, secure bottom square to serving surface with strips of icing.) Pipe icing along bottom and side edges of side rectangles. Join sides to bottom. Place heavy objects (such as 15-ounce canned food items) along outside of box to hold sides upright until icing is set and dry.

8. Decorate cut-out cookies with icing as desired. (See cover photo for ideas in icing gingerbread figures.) Stuff gift box with colored tissue paper, fill with decorated cookies, place cover on top, and tie ribbon.

Makes 1 gift box and assortment of cookies.

Tip: Look for pasteurized egg whites where you buy eggs. Because they are uncooked in this icing, regular egg whites are not recommended.

From *Christmas: The Annual of Christmas Literature and Art*, 1994, volume 64, page 62

Presents and Trees

Christmas is called *Weihnachten*, or "Watch Night," in Germany. Traditionally, in anticipation of Christmas, everyone in the household would have been very industrious making things for loved ones. One custom was to wrap the presents in various layers of wrapping paper called a *julklapp*. Each layer would bear a different person's name, until the last wrapping was opened; this final layer would bear the rightful recipient's name.

The family would arrange presents around the Christmas tree in piles, one stack for each person. As a rule, a home would have one Christmas tree, fixed on a small stand in the center of a large square table covered with a snow-white cloth. The custom of decorated Christmas trees comes from Germany. On the tree, family members usually would hang lights, glass ornaments, tinsel, a few very small toys, apples, gilded nuts, and sweets. Some of the sweets made for German trees were very elaborate. There were *kringel*—transparent sugar cookies twisted in figure eights or circles, so they would easily hang on a tree. And there were sugar candy animals of every shape and color.

Honig Kuchen

A glazed, citrus-and-spice cookie

Cookies

2 ⅔ cups blanched almonds, divided
2 tablespoons finely chopped candied citron
1 tablespoon grated orange peel
1 tablespoon grated lemon peel
1 cup honey
1 cup sugar
2 tablespoons orange juice
2 cups all-purpose flour
½ teaspoon salt
¼ teaspoon ground cinnamon
¼ teaspoon ground cloves
¼ teaspoon ground nutmeg
¼ teaspoon ground allspice

Glaze

1 cup powdered sugar
1 teaspoon grated orange peel
1 to 2 tablespoons orange juice

Special equipment

Cookie cutter

1. Place 2 cups of the almonds in food processor bowl; process until ground. Add citron, orange and lemon peels; process until well combined.

2. In large bowl, combine honey, sugar, and orange juice; mix well. Stir in almond mixture until well blended. Add all remaining cookie ingredients; mix well. Cover and refrigerate 1 to 2 hours for easier handling.

3. Heat oven to 325°F. Grease cookie sheets. On lightly floured surface, roll dough to ⅛-inch thickness. Cut with floured 2-inch heart-shaped cookie cutter. Place on cookie sheet. Top each cookie with whole almond.

4. Bake 8 to 10 minutes or until golden brown. Cool completely. In medium bowl, mix powdered sugar, 1 teaspoon orange peel, and enough orange juice for desired drizzling consistency. Drizzle glaze over cooled cookies.

Makes about 3 dozen cookies.

From *Christmas: The Annual of Christmas Literature and Art*, 1963, volume 33, page 62

Announcing Christmas

Sometime after the first snowfall in Hungary, the red hoods of Father Winter would traditionally begin appearing in shop windows, and the fir trees would arrive from the mountains to fill homes with Christmas beauty. Then it would be time to do the holiday baking.

Estike (Evening Fairies) were a favorite Hungarian Christmas cookie. Because the cookies must sit out overnight to become crisp, people believed that fairies came to taste the cookies and keep watch over them.

*Estike**

Light, lemon- and-anise-flavored treats called "Evening Fairies"

Cookies

2 eggs
½ cup sugar
1 tablespoon lemon juice
1 teaspoon vanilla
⅔ cup all-purpose flour
⅛ teaspoon salt
¼ teaspoon anise seed

1. Using mixer, beat eggs in large bowl about 5 minutes or until thick and lemon-colored. Gradually add sugar, beating constantly until well blended.

2. Add lemon juice and vanilla; beat well. Add flour and salt; mix well. Cover loosely with plastic wrap; refrigerate 8 hours or overnight.

3. Line cookie sheets with parchment paper. Drop by teaspoonfuls onto paper. Sprinkle each cookie with two or three anise seeds.

4. Heat oven to 300°F. Bake cookies 12 to 15 minutes or until dry but not brown. Remove from cookie sheets; cool on wire racks.

Makes about 5 dozen cookies.

**Tip: This is pronounced esh-TEE-keh.*

From *Christmas: The Annual of Christmas Literature and Art*, 1991, volume 61, page 30

Symbolizing the Christmas Story

In Russia, one Christmas legend tells of old *Baboushka*, "grandmother," who is said to have misdirected the Wise Men when they inquired the way to Bethlehem. She repented the next day but since then is thought to be roaming the world looking for the child Jesus. She tries to make amends by giving gifts to children.

On Christmas Eve, before the *kolydaki*, "carols," and the *badynak*, "burning log," the Russian people traditionally celebrated the meal known as the "holy supper." The entire day was spent preparing the foods. A place was set for any family members who died or had to be away from home. Shades were drawn and a single candle was lit in the center of the white tablecloth to signify the star of Bethlehem.

Before the meal began, the father served a wafer of bread, imprinted with nativity scenes as a symbol of love and peace, to his wife and children. Twelve courses were eaten one by one in honor of the twelve apostles who proclaimed the gospel. The meal began with a bitter taste of garlic, *chesnok*, to remind the family of the bitterness of the world before Christ came, and it ended with sweets.

Miatniye Prianiki*

Round peppermint-flavored cookies, perfect with tea

Cookies

1 cup milk
½ teaspoon hartshorn (ammonium bicarbonate)**
1 cup sugar
1 tablespoon vegetable oil
8 drops peppermint oil
3 ¼ cups all-purpose flour
Dash salt

1. Heat oven to 350°F. Grease cookie sheets. Heat milk in small saucepan just until bubbles begin to appear on surface. (Do not boil.)

2. In large bowl, combine milk and hartshorn; mix well. Add sugar, vegetable oil, and peppermint oil. Add flour and salt; mix well. With floured hands, roll dough into 1-inch balls. Place 2 inches apart on greased cookie sheets.

3. Bake 10 to 12 minutes or until set. (Cookies should not brown.) Remove from cookie sheets; cool on wire racks.

Makes about 3 ½ dozen cookies.

Tip: This is pronounced mee-Yaht-nee-yeh pree-AH-nee-kee.

**Tip: Hartshorn, a white powder available at most drugstores, is used as a leavening agent in these cookies. The predecessor of baking powder and baking soda, hartshorn is still called for in some cookie recipes as it provides a "fluffiness" that the other agents do not. If your drugstore carries this in granular form, be sure to grind it to a fine powder before using. It may give off an ammonia odor while the dough is raw or baking, but this will not be smelled or tasted in the cookies themselves. If you are unable to find hartshorn, you may substitute an equal amount of baking powder, but your cookies might not be as light or crisp.*

From *Christmas: The Annual of Christmas Literature and Art*, 1991, volume 61, page 31

My Family Favorites

My Family Favorites

My Family Favorites

_____
_____
_____
_____
_____
_____
_____
_____
_____
_____
_____
_____
_____
_____
_____
_____
_____
_____

My Family Favorites

—◆—

_____

_____

_____

_____

_____

_____

_____

_____

_____

_____

_____

_____

_____

_____

_____

_____

_____

_____

Index

Sources

Information for the stories in this cookbook came from the following articles in *Christm* *The Annual of Christmas Literature and Art.*

Campbell, Suzanne P., "Legends and Lore of the Yuletide Tree," 1990, volume 60, page

Campbell, Suzanne P., "Visions of Sugar Plums," 1991, volume 61, pages 26-31.

Dobrik, Peter, translated by Anne Jordheim, "The Christkindles Market," 1965, volume page 63.

Evelyn, Melva R., "The Christmas Kitchen," 1963, volume 33, page 63.

Faris, John T., "Christmas in America," 1935, volume 5, page 23.

"Germany," 1959, volume 29, page 41.

Haddock, Patricia, "Traditions in Common," 1988, volume 58, page 32.

Jensen, Grace Jewel, "Yuletide Traditions and Customs," 1938, volume 8, pages 25-28.

Klug, Ron, "The Christmas Crib," 1982, volume 52, pages 14-17.

Meyer, Marie Malmin, "Christmas in Scandinavia," 1952, volume 22, pages 18, 21.

Mueller, Agnes Harrigan, "International Christmas Trees," 1957, volume 27, pages 28-2

Nelson, Daniel, "Ten Million, Ten Million," 1934, volume 4, page 44.

Olson, Karen F., "Christmas in Many Lands," 1973, volume 43, pages 39, 42.

Peterson, James, "Season of Joy in Mexico," 1989, volume 59, page 49.

Poovey, W.A., "Symbols Tell the Christmas Story," 1982, volume 52, pages 59-60.

Rippley, La Vern J., "Children Celebrate Christmas," 1981, volume 51, pages 34, 37.

Rippley, La Vern J., "Luther's Influence on the Customs of Christmas," 1983, volume 5

Rippley, La Vern J., "The Feast of Lights," 1983, volume 53, pages 44, 46.

Rippley, La Vern J., "Twelve Days of Christmas," 1985, volume 55, pages 53-58.

Rippley, La Vern J., "Christmas on the Baltic," 1987, volume 57, page 47.

Rorem, Melva, "Customs of Christmas," 1970, volume 40, pages 47, 49-50.

Rorem, Melva, "Christmas Customs," 1971, volume 41, page 31.

Rorem, Melva, "Peace on Earth Good Will to All," 1985, volume 55, page 45.

Rulon, Philip Reed, "The Decorated Tree," 1990, volume 60, page 53.

Sevold, Ann R., "Christmas Customs Around the World," 1967, volume 37, pages 51-5

Slattery, Marianne, "Favorite American Carols," 1990, volume 60, page 41.

Smith, Jean Louise, "Christmas in Little Denmark," 1977, volume 47, page 48.

Wisner, Donald W., "Eastern Orthodox Christmas," 1986, volume 56, pages 19-20.

Wyly, Louise B., "Christmas Customs in South America," 1989, volume 59, pages 17-2